Business and Management in the Age of Intangible Capitalism

Business and Management in the Age of Intangible Capitalism

Hamid Yeganeh

BEP

BUSINESS EXPERT PRESS

Leader in applied, concise business books

Business and Management in the Age of Intangible Capitalism

Cover design by Brent Beckley

Interior design by Exeter Premedia Services Private Ltd., Chennai, India

First published in 2024 by
Business Expert Press, LLC
222 East 46th Street, New York, NY 10017
www.businessexpertpress.com

ISBN-13: 978-1-63742-718-7 (paperback)
ISBN-13: 978-1-63742-719-4 (e-book)

Business Expert Press Human Resource Management and Organizational Behavior Collection

First edition: 2024

10 9 8 7 6 5 4 3 2 1

Description

The rise of intangible capitalism is a complex socio-economic phenomenon that has gained momentum in recent years, as 90 percent of the value of S&P 500 companies consists of intangible assets. The prevalence of intangible capitalism represents a paradigmatic shift, suggesting a departure from conventional business practices for multiple compelling reasons. The change affects fundamental aspects of business, including strategies, competitive advantages, organizational structures, investment practices, marketing approaches, and even business valuations. Furthermore, intangible assets, directly or indirectly, have substantial implications for society and our daily lives.

Business and Management in the Age of Intangible Capitalism focuses on intangible assets and their repercussions for business and society. It provides insights into the evolving landscape of intangible capitalism, where wealth generation is increasingly based on invisible elements.

This volume serves as a critical resource for managers, scholars, and citizens navigating the complexities of the modern intangible economy.

Contents

Introduction

The rise of intangible capitalism is a complex socio-economic phenomenon that has gained momentum in recent years. Based on some recent estimates, 90 percent of the value of S&P 500 companies consists of intangible assets. This shift can be attributed to various factors, including human development, globalization, technological progress, and evolving economic structures. In intangible capitalism, economic value is generated by manipulating ideas rather than transforming physical assets. Intangible assets refer to a broad category of nonphysical assets such as intellectual properties, brand values, human capital, trade secrets, and unidentifiable assets such as goodwill. Intangible assets, in contrast to tangible assets, exhibit distinct economic characteristics. They invariably involve knowledge content and are characterized by nonscarcity, limited tradability, high levels of scalability, spillover, sunk costs, synergies, risk, network effects, and uncertainty.

The prevalence of intangible capitalism represents a paradigmatic shift, suggesting a departure from conventional business practices for multiple compelling reasons. As the significance of intangibles continues to increase, fundamental aspects such as business strategies, competitive advantages, organizational structures, investment practices, marketing approaches, and even business valuations undergo profound transformations. Furthermore, intangible assets, directly or indirectly, have substantial implications for society and our daily lives as citizens.

Considering the rising significance of intangible assets, the current volume explores the concept of intangible assets and its consequences for different areas of business and society. The book is structured in two major parts. Part 1 is dedicated to the concept of intangible assets. The first part is organized into five chapters and explores the phenomenal growth of intangible assets, their causes and antecedents, definitions, typologies, and characteristics. The second part, which is more practical, focuses on the implications of intangible capitalism for different areas of business, from organization and management to accounting, finance, and marketing. Additionally, the last chapter reflects on the societal impacts of intangible capitalism and how it affects social values, attitudes, behaviors, and cognitions.

PART 1

Understanding the Intangible Capitalism

CHAPTER 1

The Rise of Intangibles

Wealth Is Invisible!

Introduction

This chapter highlights the phenomenal rise of intangible assets in the modern economy. Once we grasp the increasing prevalence of intangible assets on firms' balance sheets, it becomes apparent that these transformations are not just about numbers. Instead, this trend represents a fundamental shift that permeates all industries and sectors. The rise of intangible assets embodies a monumental paradigm shift in the global economic landscape, challenging and redefining traditional notions of wealth and value creation. We understand that wealth is becoming increasingly immaterial in the new intangible capitalism. Furthermore, we learn that while intangible assets prominently feature in the information and telecommunication sectors, their impact extends across various industries. Intangible assets enhance the performance of firms and present significant challenges and ramifications.

The Phenomenal Rise of Intangible Assets

Until about three decades ago, businesses primarily channeled their investments into tangible assets such as land, buildings, machinery, and material resources. This trend, rooted in the Industrial Revolution, persisted until the late 20th century. However, starting in the 1990s, marked by the collapse of the Soviet Union and the widespread use of personal computers, a significant transformation occurred, leading to a pronounced surge in investments in intangible or immaterial assets. The 1990s marked the beginning of a new era characterized by high technology, digitalization, and globalization, with intangible assets assuming a predominant role. An illustration of this change can be observed in the evolution of the balance sheets of S&P 500 companies in the past five decades (see Figures 1.1 and 1.2). In 1975, the value of intangible assets in these companies amounted to a modest $122 billion. However, by 1995, this figure had skyrocketed to $3.12 trillion; by 2018, it had surpassed a staggering $21.03 trillion. The shift was so profound that current estimates suggest intangible assets now constitute a whopping 90 percent of the total assets in the S&P 500 index [11].

Tangible assets are rising to the detriment of tangibles. The diminishing significance of tangible assets is highlighted by the drastic change in their value relative to market value. For instance, between 1982 and 1999, the proportion of tangible assets to market value plummeted from an average of 62 percent to a mere 15 percent, showcasing the waning importance of physical assets in the overall valuation of companies [6]. In 1995, tangible investments still dominated the scene, with a split of 70 percent for tangible assets and 30 percent for intangibles. However, the landscape underwent a substantial transformation by 2019, with the split shifting to 60 percent for tangibles and 40 percent for intangibles, signifying a substantial tilt toward the latter [6].

The evolution of the shift to intangibles is strikingly illustrated by the changing composition of a firm's assets. In 1978, intangible assets comprised a mere 5 percent of all assets, with conventional accounting assets taking precedence. Fast forward to 2008, and the landscape had undergone a remarkable transformation, with intangible assets representing a staggering 78 percent of all assets, relegating traditional physical assets to a marginal role [3]. Despite temporary setbacks, notably in the aftermath of the 2008 global financial crisis, the momentum of this trend not only recovered but gained further impetus during the economic downturn induced by the COVID-19 pandemic. Instead of impeding the trajectory of intangible investments, the pandemic acted as a catalyst, amplifying the recognition of their strategic importance. The surge in remote working and the accelerated pace of digitalization during social distancing measures highlighted the critical role of intangibles in adapting to and thriving in an increasingly dynamic and uncertain business environment.

This transformative trend is not confined to a specific geography. However, it is evident across various countries, showcasing a global shift toward prioritizing intangible investments over tangible ones. According to the McKinsey Global Institute report [8], by 2019, intangible assets accounted for a substantial 40 percent of total investment in the United States and 10 European economies, marking a significant increase from 29 percent in 1995. In the United States, recent studies estimate an annual investment in intangibles ranging between $800 billion and $1 trillion, resulting in a substantial stock of intangibles valued at up to $5 trillion [1]. Similarly, in the United Kingdom, investment in intangibles has more than doubled as a proportion of market sector gross value added between 1970 and 2004 [1].

The shift in the composition of investments signals a profound change in the nature of assets valued by businesses, with a clear departure from the traditionally dominant physical and tangible assets toward those that are intangible. It reflects a strategic realignment wherein organizations recognize the importance of intangible assets in navigating the complexities of the contemporary business landscape and ensuring long-term competitiveness and success.

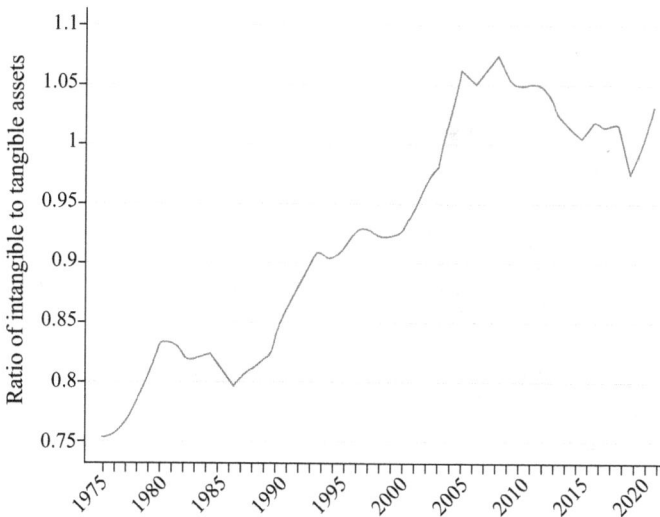

Figure 1.1 Ratio of intangible assets to tangible assets for U.S. public firms, 1975–2021

Source: [5]

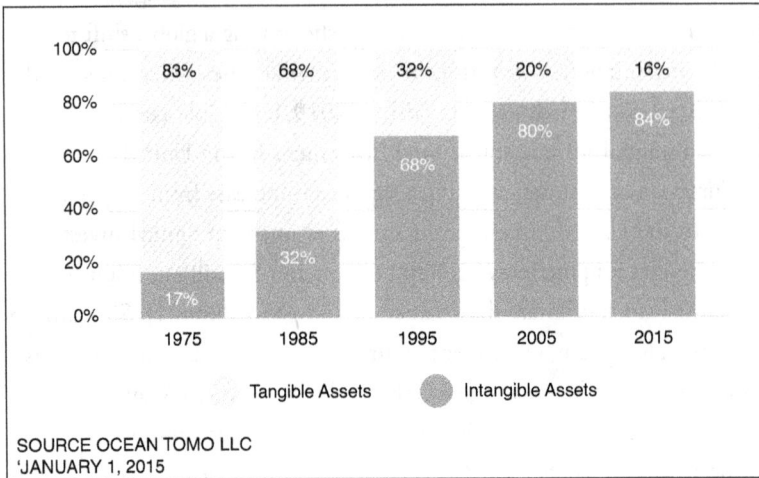

Figure 1.2 Components of S&P 500 market value

Source: [7]

A Paradigmatic Shift

The rise of intangible assets represents a monumental paradigm shift in the global economic landscape, challenging and redefining traditional notions of wealth and value creation. A transformative evolution has occurred, ushering in an era characterized by the primacy of technology, innovation, creativity, and services. In this new paradigm, the creation of wealth has moved from the control of tangible resources to a landscape where the manipulation of ideas is the primary driver of prosperity. The World Bank estimates that intangible capital now constitutes the predominant form of global wealth, departing from conventional measures focused solely on tangible resources.

The relationship between investment in intangibles and critical business outcomes is vividly illustrated by the example of the United Kingdom in 2004. The direct attribution of approximately half of the export sales from recipients of the Queen's Award for Exports to investments in design exemplifies the strategic impact of intangible assets on global competitiveness and international success [1]. It highlights that intangible investments, particularly in areas such as design, have intense and far-reaching effects on a company's ability to thrive in the global market.

The rise of intangible investments indicates a new era where companies derive value from producing and selling physical goods and from creating, protecting, and exploiting intangible assets. In this globalized, digitalized, and knowledge-driven world, the strategic management of intangible assets has become closely linked with corporate returns, productivity, and economic growth. As a result of this paradigm shift, operational structures are now more flexible, with strategic decisions influenced by the availability of talented labor and valuable technological partnerships. The intangibles of knowledge and innovation-based relationships contribute to shaping the dynamics of these modern economies, dispersing operations beyond visible arenas. Terms such as the "information revolution" and "knowledge-based economy" encapsulate the essence of these transformations, reshaping industries from centralized giants to widely dispersed operations.

The concept of the intangible economy extends its impact across every sector and facet of economic activities. Unlike historical shifts that phased out sectors like agriculture during the Industrial Revolution, the intangible economy does not eliminate traditional sectors but reshapes the fundamental logic underpinning economic relationships. The locus of economic value creation decisively shifts toward intangible assets, emphasizing the transformative role of knowledge, innovation, and intangible content.

In this intangible economy, aspects such as user experience, branding, and ecosystems take precedence, suggesting a departure from the traditional focus on physical goods. Information is no longer a supplementary element but the primary driver of value, revolutionizing how businesses operate and compete. The transition from agrarian and industrial economies to intangible economies is not just a shift in production methods but a comprehensive and enduring transformation that impacts the core of economic activity across diverse sectors. This evolution means a new era where economic value is generated through the complex interactions between humans and abstract ideas.

Intangible Assets and Business Performance

There is a significant relationship between the allocation of resources to intangible assets and the overall performance, growth, and competitiveness of businesses across diverse sectors. For instance, companies with a remarkable median growth rate of 20 percent in 2018 to 2019 demonstrated a substantial commitment to investing in intangible assets, diverging notably from their lower-performing counterparts with a median growth rate of 3 percent [8]. Studies have quantified the impact of previously unmeasured intangible capital on economic productivity, accounting for 18 percent of the growth in multifactor productivity in the United States between the mid-1990s and early 2000s [1]. Many surveys and investigations affirm a consensus among top and low growers across sectors about the critical role of intangible assets in fostering growth and competitiveness. For instance, in some surveys, approximately 24 percent strongly agree that digital and analytics capital is crucial for sustainable competitive advantage, spanning sectors like telecommunications, media, technology, and advanced manufacturing [8]. These observations highlight a strong relationship between intangible investments and the overall performance of businesses. High-performing businesses, especially in knowledge-centric sectors like financial services, exhibited a considerable investment gap compared to their lower-performing counterparts [4]. In these sectors, top-performing companies invested between five and seven times more in intangibles, emphasizing the crucial role of knowledge as a primary competitive advantage. A consistent correlation between effective adaptation to the intangible trend and superior business outcomes further highlights the strategic importance of intangible assets in enhancing business performance. Companies in the top quartile of gross value-added growth invest 2.6 times more in intangibles than their low-growth counterparts, reinforcing the argument that deliberate investments in intangibles significantly contribute to sustained growth [8].

Despite the economic challenges posed by the COVID-19 crisis, evidence suggests that intangible assets may have been pivotal in fostering a resilient economic recovery. The pandemic prompted businesses to accelerate their efforts in digitization and automation in response to lockdowns and reduced demand. Survey data supported this trend, revealing heightened expectations for increased investments in new technologies in the next five years. The link between investment in intangible assets and heightened growth, especially where knowledge is a critical competitive advantage, is undeniable. The observed disparities in investment practices between high and low performers underline the strategic significance of intangible capital in steering business success and resilience, even in the face of significant economic disruptions.

The evolving business and industry landscape exhibits a profound shift toward recognizing and prioritizing intangible assets due to their direct correlation with company performance. This transformation is acknowledged across diverse industries, leading companies to allocate more significant portions of their budgets to research and development (R&D). The primary objective of this increased investment is to stimulate innovation, generate new technologies, and build intellectual property (IP). At the same time, companies actively seek legal protection for their innovations, contributing to the expansion of extensive IP portfolios and emphasizing the growing role of IP as a valuable intangible asset.

Once considered merely marketing elements, brands have evolved into crucial intangible assets. Valuations of brands, often comprising consumer perception, brand loyalty, and market position, have experienced significant appreciation. Some of the world's most valuable companies now derive a substantial portion of their market capitalization from the strength of their brands. The acknowledgment of human capital as a pivotal intangible asset has seen a noteworthy rise. Companies increasingly recognize that their workforce's skills, knowledge, and expertise significantly contribute to organizational success. Investments in employee training, development, and retention reflect the growing importance assigned to human capital. The digital age has ushered in an era of data as a valuable intangible asset. Companies not only amass extensive amounts of data but also develop capabilities to analyze and derive insights from it. Data-driven decision making has emerged as a strategic advantage, further propelling data growth as an intangible asset. Industries are transitioning toward service-oriented business models, where customer relationships, brand reputation, and proprietary software take center stage.

The growth of intangible assets is not confined to individual companies; it influences overall economic output and productivity. In the knowledge-based economy, industries effectively leveraging intangible assets tend to exhibit higher productivity levels, contributing significantly to economic growth. Investors are adjusting their focus, emphasizing intangible assets more when evaluating companies' value and growth potential. This shift reflects an understanding that intangible assets contribute significantly to a company's competitive advantage and long-term sustainability. Governments and regulatory bodies are adapting policies to accommodate the increasing importance of intangible assets. Changes in accounting standards and IP laws are being implemented to ensure that the value of intangible assets is appropriately recognized and protected. As the knowledge-based economy continues to evolve, the growth of intangible assets is expected to persist, shaping the strategies and competitiveness of firms across various sectors.

It is important to note that the value and productivity of intangibles involve substantial upfront investments that may take time to yield results. These investments are not easily recoverable, and the risk of intangible assets being copied or stolen adds to the complexity. However, two fundamental characteristics make the upfront investment worthwhile: scalability and synergies. Intangibles can be scaled globally, as seen in the development of brands like Coca-Cola. Additionally, they offer synergies, where investments in human capital, for example, can attract and retain talent, providing a competitive edge in valuable digital and analytical know-how. Examples like BioNTech's investment in developing a COVID-19 vaccine and Amazon's and Netflix's efforts in personalization highlight that the considerable upfront costs of intangible investments contribute to building assets that can be as valuable, if not more valuable, than traditional tangible assets like factories. Despite the risk of copying, the scalability and synergies associated with intangibles make them valuable and integral to creating enduring competitive advantages in the modern business landscape.

The Case of the Information and Communication Technology Sector

Investments in intangible assets exhibit distinct trends, with the information and communication technology sector standing out as a prominent player over the past 25 years. Renowned for its innovation-driven services, this sector has consistently introduced disruptive innovations, particularly in the last decade, expanding platforms and markets on an unprecedented scale. Noteworthy examples include groundbreaking ventures such as Apple's iOS and app store and the widely embraced

Amazon Prime. The information and communication technology sector has directed a significant portion of its investments toward innovation capital and digital and analytics capital, surpassing sector averages by a considerable margin.

Complex Consequences of the Rise of Intangibles

The emergence of intangible assets represents a complex phenomenon with profound implications spanning various dimensions, including investment patterns, economic stabilities, growth, monetary policies, and employment dynamics. Contrary to the common belief attributing the surge in intangible investment solely to tech giants like Amazon, Apple, and Google, its roots extend beyond the technology sector. Diverse industries, from retail and manufacturing to education and health care, have experienced transformative shifts contributing to this trend. For example, consider the retail sector, traditionally grounded in physical assets. Today, most of their investments are directed toward intangibles, reflecting a broader shift in strategic priorities. The rapid growth of the information technology and professional service sectors has been a critical driver of this transformation. Sectors like professional and information services have experienced substantial expansion and considerably impacted employment and the overall share of gross domestic product (GDP).

The surge in intangible investment has surpassed the combined investment shares of more traditional sectors like agriculture, mining, and construction, signaling a fundamental reorientation in the composition of investments. An analysis of different investment categories' contribution to real GDP growth shows the stability provided by intangible investment compared to equipment and structures. Even during the turbulent period of the Great Recession, intangible investment exhibited minimal negative impact on GDP growth, contributing to a more stable economic environment [9].

The existing policy tools, such as interest and tax rates, designed for a tangible economy, need to be revised to manage this intangibles-focused environment. Traditional economic strategies, including foreign direct investment (FDI) and global supply chain optimization, are being overshadowed by the imperative to secure "freedom to operate" in IP and data [2]. The rise of the intangible economy has profound implications for monetary policy. Traditionally, central banks influence investment patterns through changes in interest rates. However, the increasing dominance of intangible investment presents challenges to this conventional approach. Research suggests that intangible investment is less responsive to monetary policy due to distinct financing costs and depreciation rates. Financing primarily through internal cash holdings and higher depreciation rates renders intangible investments less sensitive to fluctuations in interest rates [9, 10]. The user cost of capital, encapsulating financing costs and depreciation rates, plays a pivotal role in shaping investment decisions. Changes in financing costs, influenced by the reliance on bank loans, impact the sensitivity of investment to interest rates. Intangible investments, often funded through internal resources, exhibit lower sensitivity. Furthermore, the faster depreciation of intangible assets contributes to reduced responsiveness to monetary policy [9].

The rise of mega-firms in the intangibles economy, characterized by minimal taxes, reduced capital expenditure, and reliance on global-scale operations, has necessitated reevaluating economic policies. The profound consequences of data control extend beyond economics, impacting social, political, and geopolitical spheres. Data governance has become a critical public policy issue, demanding strategic responses at the company and state levels [2].

The international competitive landscape has radically transformed with the rise of the intangibles economy. The United States recognized the importance of IP early on, leveraging it to become a dominant force int the global economy. Other nations, notably China, implemented comprehensive strategies to raise their game in the IP and data-intensive economy, leading to significant global technology competitiveness [2].

Concluding Remarks

This chapter offered an overview of the emergence of intangible capitalism, emphasizing its profound impact across various business domains. In Chapter 2, we explore this phenomenon further by drawing on insights from sociology, business, management, and cultural studies to analyze the main factors of the rise of intangible capitalism.

CHAPTER 2

Explaining the Rise of Intangible Capitalism

Introduction

The rise of intangible capitalism can be attributed to many interrelated social, cultural, technological, and economic factors, collectively contributing to the changing landscape of capital allocation. An American sociologist, Daniel Bell, popularized postindustrial society to describe the significant socio-economic shifts in the late 20th century [4,5]. Exploring postindustrial society extended beyond Bell's contributions, with other notable scholars investigating the underlying factors. An influential sociologist, Anthony Giddens, examined the intersection of globalization and technological changes, explaining how these forces reshaped social structures and individual experiences [13]. In his work *Post-Capitalist Society* (2012), Peter Drucker, a prominent management authority, investigated the broader transition from an industrial to a knowledge-based economy, shedding light on the pivotal role played by knowledge workers in this evolving landscape [11]. Manuel Castells, a scholar on society and technology [10], focused on the rise of networked communication technologies and their profound effects on the global economy and society. At the same time, Ulrich Beck, a prominent German sociologist [2,3], analyzed the move toward a postindustrial society, scrutinizing associated risks and technological hazards. In his seminal modernization theory, Ronald Inglehart [16, 17] contributed significantly by highlighting the shift from industrial/materialist to postindustrial/postmaterialist values and exploring their implications for politics and culture. In this chapter, we analyze the drivers behind the rise of the intangible economy from different perspectives.

The Postindustrial Society as the Basis of Intangible Capitalism

The transition toward an intangible economy, a process unfolding over several decades, was notably expressed by Daniel Bell [4] in his seminal work *The Coming of Post-Industrial Society: A Venture in Social Forecasting*. Bell played a pivotal role in introducing the concept during a period when traditional industrial economies, characterized by manufacturing and manual labor, were undergoing profound transformations. Bell observed a shift from economies dominated by manufacturing and industry to those where the service sector and information-based activities took center stage. This marked a departure from the industrial era's emphasis on production and manual labor, as service-oriented professions gradually replaced traditional manufacturing jobs. A central theme in Bell's theory highlighted the increasing importance of information and knowledge as crucial drivers of economic productivity. The rise of technological advancements, particularly in automation and information technology, diminished the demand for manual labor in manufacturing and intensified the need for knowledge-based professions. This showed the critical roles of education, research, and information technology in shaping the emerging economic landscape [4,5].

As early as the 1970s, Bell predicted the rise in significance of intellectual and service professions involving areas such as education, research, finance, and technology. These sectors were viewed as pivotal contributors to economic growth, with the expertise and knowledge they offered becoming increasingly valuable in a postindustrial society. Technological innovation, especially automation, was recognized by Bell for its transformative impact on the nature of work. Automating industrial processes led to a decline in the demand for manual labor in manufacturing, prompting a shift toward more automated and technologically driven production methods.

Bell's theory emphasized the broader cultural and social changes happening with the transition to a postindustrial society. This incorporated a transformation in societal values, emphasizing individualism, personal development, and the pursuit of knowledge and information.

The concept of a postindustrial society gained substantial prominence in the 1990s, coinciding with the widespread adoption of terms such as globalization, outsourcing, network society, automation, information highway, and instant telecommunication. Multinational corporations responded to this shift by globally decentralizing their value chain activities [15]. Pivotal moments during the dot-com bubble in the early 2000s and the 2007 financial crisis marked critical milestones in this trajectory. Despite economic challenges, the world economy experienced remarkable growth, particularly in the information technology sector, propelling further into postindustrialization and digitalization. This phase was characterized by substantial investments in intangible assets, highlighting the increasing significance of knowledge and information in driving economic productivity and societal advancement.

Bell's conceptualization of a postindustrial society significantly influenced discussions on the changing nature of work, the economy, and societal structures. While certain aspects of his theory have been subject to debate and evolving interpretations, the core ideas remain instrumental in explaining the transformations witnessed in Western societies over the past four decades.

Human Development Sequence and Intangible Economy

The concept of the human development sequence, as outlined by the modernization theory and discussed by Inglehart and Welzel [18], offers a helpful framework for understanding the shifting priorities of individuals in different stages of economic development. Inglehart and Welzel's theory, particularly their human development sequence, is closely related to the transition from industrial to postindustrial societies. The theory provides insights into how cultural values evolve as societies undergo modernization, economic development, and social change.

In the early phases of modernization, societies are characterized by an emphasis on materialist values (industrial or manufacturing economy). These values prioritize economic stability, security, and order. Traditional structures and norms tend to dominate, reflecting the challenges and priorities associated with industrialization. As societies progress through the stages of modernization, particularly in the transition to postindustrialism, there is a notable shift in values accordingly. Postindustrial societies, marked by advanced technological and economic development, witness a move from materialist values to postmaterialist values. This transition is associated with the emergence of self-expression values, emphasizing individual autonomy, political participation, and the importance of human rights. In postindustrial societies, where information technology, service-based industries, and knowledge play a central role in the economy, the human development sequence predicts the prevalence of self-expression values. Inglehart and Welzel argue that societies in the advanced stages of modernization are more likely to prioritize nonmaterial concerns such as quality of life, personal fulfillment, and the protection of individual rights. Thus, according to Inglehart and Welzel [18], individuals in economically advanced societies tend to transition toward higher needs associated with less tangible production. This progression aligns with Maslow's hierarchy of needs [25], which suggests that once basic needs are met, individuals seek to fulfill higher-order needs related to self-actualization, personal growth, and experiences. Consistent with Maslow's perspective, the human development sequence posits that, in affluent societies, there is a notable shift in consumer preferences from essential material goods toward services and consumption experiences. In other words, as societies become more economically developed, individuals allocate more resources toward services that enhance their quality of life. This shift is noticeable in increased spending on experiences, health care, education, entertainment, and other services.

The transition from prioritizing survival values to emphasizing higher-order needs mirrors a broader societal evolution associated with economic development. This shift influences individual consumption patterns and contributes to the transformation of societal values, lifestyles, and preferences. In developed economies, the focus on services and intangible aspects of life becomes more pronounced, reflecting a stage of development where basic material needs are largely satisfied. This analysis of the human development sequence highlights the interconnectedness between economic development, individual priorities, and societal values. It provides a lens through which to understand how, as societies progress economically, there is a corresponding evolution in the preferences and aspirations of individuals, aligning with the broader trajectory of human development.

Globalization as a Driver of Intangible Capitalism

Giddens views globalization as a complex and transformative process that intensifies and expands worldwide social relations and interdependence [13]. Globalization entails a heightened level of interconnectedness among nations and individuals on a global scale, encompassing economic, political, and sociocultural dimensions [2, 13]. Globalization has historical roots but has gained significant prominence in contemporary discourse, particularly during the latter part of the 20th century. From an economic perspective, globalization means a departure from the traditional model of self-contained national economies. Instead, it heralds the emergence of a global marketplace where production, distribution, and consumption transcend national borders, allowing goods and services to originate from diverse corners of the world.

The globalization of markets involves the globalization of the world's national markets. It entails the increasing convergence of consumer preferences in markets worldwide. The globalization of markets is affecting the majority of consumer goods, including food, clothing, electronics, and automobiles. Giant multinational corporations like Coca-Cola, McDonald's, Starbucks, and Apple are overcoming national borders by offering their products and services to different countries. As such, every citizen of the world, regardless of nationality or location, is a potential customer of such corporations. Today's industries, such as music streaming, microprocessors, aircraft, construction equipment, online retail, automobiles, financial services, business consulting, and consumer goods, embody global markets, products, and competition. The ability to operate globally has increased the significance of intangible assets. Brands, digital platforms, and intellectual property can reach a global audience more quickly, allowing companies to expand their market presence and customer base [9]. The market size plays a pivotal role in shaping intangible investment dynamics. Certain intangible assets, such as brands and software, can scale infinitely. Smaller markets with trade barriers tend to impose limitations on intangible investment opportunities [14]. Thus, the growing global markets have immensely benefited intangible assets in the past three decades.

Globalization, or global production, refers to the practice of dispersing or decentralizing various stages of the production process for goods and services to different locations around the world. It involves strategically allocating production activities to specific geographic locations, considering cost efficiency, resource availability, expertise, and market proximity. The globalization of production has been driven by advances in technology, transportation, and communication, which have made it easier for companies to invest in intangible assets and manage and coordinate production activities across borders. This strategy enables businesses to remain competitive in a globalized world by capitalizing on nonmaterial and intangible assets and taking advantage of different regional endowments. Thus, the globalization of production has made it easier for companies to sell manufactured products without engaging in their manufacturing directly.

Some *factory-free* producers like Apple provide good examples as they sell and organize the production of manufacturing goods without being involved in the actual production process [7, 12]. They provide intangible assets, including software and designs, market knowledge, intellectual property, systems integration, cost management, and a strong brand name. However, we cannot determine the amount of income that is generated by these *intangibles* in national accounts statistics as their use cannot be attributed to a geographical location. However, tangible assets (such as machinery) and labor have physical elements, and their use is recorded in the national account statistics of the countries where they are located. Because of the globalization of production, many manufacturing jobs have been offshored to countries with cheaper labor, leading to a decline in the manufacturing sector in developed countries.

Technology and Digitalization as Drivers of Intangible Capitalism

The rapid development of technology, particularly in information technology and telecommunications, has ushered in a transformative era in the business landscape. This evolution has been pivotal in the rise of intangible assets, marking a profound economic value shift from traditional tangible to intangible ones. This shift characterizes the automation of manufacturing processes, heightened efficiency, and reduced reliance on manual labor.

Intangible assets like data, software development, and online platforms have become focal points for investment and value creation in the contemporary business environment. The emergence of the intangible economy is intricately tied to the advancements in digital technology, which have fundamentally altered how businesses operate and derive value.

One of the primary drivers of this shift is the capacity of digital technology to create, store, and retrieve vast amounts of information. This capability significantly enhances knowledge management within organizations, with data and information serving as valuable intangible assets. Businesses can utilize these assets to make informed decisions, optimize processes, and gain a competitive advantage in the market.

Investments in data analytics, machine learning, and artificial intelligence (AI) have become increasingly prevalent as companies seek to extract meaningful insights from the abundance of available data. These technologies enable more accurate predictions and improved decision-making processes and provide a competitive advantage by uncovering patterns and trends that might be overlooked through traditional means.

The value in the intangible economy is further emphasized by the digital transformation's impact on industries. The shift from physical goods to software and digital content is evident across various sectors, with the software industry experiencing substantial growth and becoming a critical component in areas like health care and finance.

The role of digital technology in creating, protecting, and exploiting IP cannot be overstated. Patents, trademarks, copyrights, and trade secrets are now considered essential assets in the intangible economy. Companies that excel in innovation and possess valuable IP often gain a competitive advantage, and digital tools play a crucial role in accelerating innovation cycles and fostering continuous improvement.

The rise of digital platforms, exemplified by tech giants like Google, Amazon, and Apple, has introduced new avenues for value creation. These platforms facilitate the exchange of goods, services, and information, generating synergies and network effects that enhance their overall value. User-generated content on these platforms adds additional intangible value, creating a dynamic and rich ecosystem. Data has emerged as a strategic asset in the economy. Companies leverage data for targeted marketing, personalization of services, and optimization of operations.

Moreover, digital technology has interconnected the global econo-mies, enabling unified operations across borders. E-commerce and digital transactions have become significant drivers of economic activity, with online platforms and marketplaces facilitating the exchange of digital goods and services. This interconnectedness contributes significantly to the growth of the intangible economy, emphasizing the importance of digital technologies in shaping the contemporary business landscape.

Environmental Concerns as Drivers of Intangible Capitalism

The manufacturing industry significantly contributes to global air pol-lution by releasing hazardous emissions, including volatile organic com-pounds (VOCs) and other pollutants. These emissions adversely affect human health and the environment, causing respiratory diseases, cancers, environmental degradation, and climate change. Various manufacturing businesses are associated with releasing pollutants such as nitrogen oxide, sulfur dioxide, carbon monoxide, particulate matter, and greenhouse gas. Controlling industrial air pollution is crucial.

Climate change is ushering in new political and economic dynam-ics globally, compelling countries and businesses to adapt. Many major corporations are incorporating climate change considerations into their business strategies, responding to pressures from regulatory bodies, envi-ronmental activists, and investors and consumers, with a focus on climate issues. While their efforts may seem progressive, a closer examination reveals that these companies are primarily committed to addressing green-house gas emissions from their production and energy consumption. They often overlook the significant indirect emissions originating from their supply chains and the use of their products, which constitute a sub-stantial portion of their total gas emissions and pollutants. Indeed, many companies decrease their local carbon footprints by relocating carbon emissions to countries with lax environmental regulations and focusing on nonpolluting, knowledge-based, and immaterial operations, including design, IP, and customer service [6, 20].

Over the past decade, the United States and Europe have made sig-nificant strides in decreasing their greenhouse gas emissions within their borders. However, these achievements are tempered by a phenomenon known as *carbon outsourcing*, where these affluent nations import carbon-intensive goods, like steel and cement, from countries with less stringent environmental regulations, such as China. This practice has allowed them to effectively *outsource* a substantial portion of their carbon pollution overseas. For instance, Britain reduced its domestic emissions by one-third between 1990 and 2015. Nevertheless, this reduction coincided with the migration of energy-intensive industries to other countries. If one were to account for the global emissions associated with the production of imported goods, such as the steel used in London's skyscrapers and cars, Britain's overall carbon footprint has experienced a slight increase over that time [23].

Regulatory Environment

IP rights (IPR) are crucial in stimulating innovation, advancing technological progress, and fostering economic growth. Recognizing the historical evolution of various IPR instruments is essential, with the overarching objective of promoting private investment in innovation and sustaining economic development. The concept of IPR serves as a fundamental catalyst for innovation by granting inventors temporary monopoly power over their creations [1, 22]. This temporary exclusivity encourages inventors to invest in new ideas and inventions, fostering a climate conducive to innovation.

Throughout history, mainly since the Industrial Revolution, there has been a concerted effort to reinforce the power of preventing others from using intellectual creations. This reinforcement strategically encourages private investment in innovation activities, thereby contributing to continuous and sustainable economic growth. Braga et al. [8] highlight that IPR also function as a regulatory framework that governs the relationships between innovators/creators and consumers. The goal is to establish a system that rewards innovators for their ideas and benefits creators and users.

Over the years, IP laws and regulations have become more robust, providing essential protection for intangible assets. This legal framework serves as a crucial incentive for companies to invest in research, innovation, and IP development, assuring them that their creations will be safeguarded. The U.S. Congress has actively taken measures to strengthen IP protections, exemplified by extensions in copyright protection from 55 to 95 years and an increase in patent protection from 14 to 20 years. These legislative actions indicate a commitment to offering more substantial and extended protection for intangible IPR.

In short, the evolution of IP laws and regulations in recent decades has resulted in a more robust framework that provides vital protection for intangible assets. This, in turn, encourages companies to commit resources to research, innovation, and IP development, as they can be confident in safeguarding their creations. The proactive stance of the U.S. Congress in enhancing patent and IP protections reinforces the value, attractiveness, and reward associated with these intangible assets. Thus, companies engage in long-term R&D projects, as the enhanced protection ensures a more favorable environment for their IP investment returns.

Other Contributing Factors and Conditions

In addition to the aforementioned factors, we may attribute the rise of intangible assets to many diverse but overlapping factors and conditions.

Urbanization and Demographic Changes

The world's population is constantly becoming more urbanized as cities are attracting a large number of inhabitants. For the first time in 2007, the world's urban population surpassed the world's rural population. According to the World Bank reports, the share of the world's urban population has risen from 30 percent in 1950 to more than 55 percent in 2018. The ongoing urbanization, in conjunction with the growth of the global population, will add 2.5 billion people to the urban population by 2050, with nearly 90 percent of the increase concentrated in Asia and Africa (Ecola et al. 2015). By 2050, almost 68 percent of the world's population will live in urban centers [27]. The trend toward urbanization has led to greater demand for services such as health care, education, entertainment, and transportation in urban areas. This effect has driven the growth of service-based industries catering to urban populations' needs. Urban centers have become hubs for knowledge-based companies and centers for producing and consuming intangible goods [24]. Furthermore, aging populations in many developed countries have led to increased demand for intangibles such as health care, medications, and elderly care.

Industrial Structure Change

Over time, services have increasingly shifted toward being more intangible-intensive. In the context of globalization, high-wage economies have directed investments toward R&D and lean production within the manufacturing sector. The complexity of modern organizations and the intricacies of globalized trade networks have further fueled the growth of intangible investments [14]. As economies transition from manufacturing-based to knowledge-based, the importance of intellectual capital and human knowledge has grown significantly. Companies that excel in research, development, and innovation gain a competitive advantage. Manufacturing is becoming an interplay between the real (material) and digital [26].

Spillover Effects and Data Analytics

In general, intangible assets benefit from network and spillover effects, where their value increases as more users or participants join. Social media platforms, online marketplaces, and communication apps are classic examples of intangible assets whose values increase over time when they become widespread. In other words, the use of intangible assets contributes to their growth. Furthermore, the availability of big data and advanced analytics tools allows companies to extract valuable insights, make data-driven decisions, and create new business opportunities. For instance, Internet-based companies such as Amazon, Meta, Google, and Uber hold enormous consumer data to create business value via big data analytics. Therefore, data itself has become a critical intangible asset.

Time–Space Compression and Economic Integration

The information revolution compresses the time–space equation, allowing for unprecedented economic integration. Manuel Castells notes that the informational economy operates globally, distinguishing it from a world economy [10]. Despite similarities with the gold standard era, economic integration is unique due to methodological differences, increased trade in goods and services, and a transformed logic of competition and integration [21]. Economic integration in postindustrial capitalism surpasses historical levels, driven by intra-industry trade, FDI, and exports of intangible capital. The logic of economic integration has shifted from an extrovert to an introvert capitalism, marked by aggressive competition within advanced economies. Multinational firms now export intangible capital, creating global networks that deepen global interdependence beyond traditional trade and FDI metrics [21].

Dematerialization and Human Capital

In the postindustrial economy, wealth accumulation shifts from goods to symbolic and relational systems. This *dematerialization* trend emphasizes the increasing importance of software, knowledge, and service relations over the material components of commodities [21]. The transition from energy-intensive to information-intensive technical systems is evident in the prevalence of electronics and information technology. This shift, described by Charles Jonscher [19], distinguishes electronics by focusing on low-power information processing rather than high-power physical work. Competent employees and knowledge workers are essential in the intangible economy. Companies that invest in recruiting, training, and, more importantly, retaining top talent can harness the full potential of their human capital. Therefore, the need for human capital and talent has led to significant investments in intangibles such as training, development, and retaining programs.

Concluding Remarks

In this chapter, we relied on various viewpoints from sociology, business, management, and cultural studies to analyze the main drivers behind the emergence of the intangible economy. We recognized that intangible capitalism is intricately linked to the socio-economic changes within modern Western societies over the last four decades. In the upcoming chapter, we will focus on the concept of an *intangible asset* and its various connotations.

CHAPTER 3

Some Tangible Meanings of Intangible Assets

Introduction

Despite its increasing importance, the concept of *intangible asset* remains nebulous as many researchers disagree on what is an intangible asset. Intangible assets, often called the hidden wealth of organizations, constitute a crucial component of modern economies. In this chapter, we explore the concept of intangible assets and explain what can be considered an intangible asset without entering into a technical debate.

The Concept of Intangible Assets

There are various definitions of intangible assets, but most remain abstract, offering limited practical guidance for practitioners or researchers. Some terminologies are interchangeable, including intangible assets, intangible capital, intangible resources, intellectual capital, and IP [8].

Generally, assets refer to everything owned economically by a company with monetary value [3]. Understanding the composition and classification of assets is essential for financial management and reporting. Different categories of assets serve distinct purposes in supporting a company's operations, growth, and strategic initiatives. We may categorize assets into four broad forms.

1. Current Assets: These are assets expected to be sold, consumed, or converted into cash within one year or the normal operating cycle of the business. Current assets consist of assets such as cash, accounts receivable, inventory, and short-term investments. They are crucial for the day-to-day operations of a company and are expected to provide liquidity.

2. Fixed Assets: Fixed assets, also known as noncurrent assets or long-term assets, include items like plant equipment, machinery, and properties that have a useful life of more than one year. Fixed assets are not generally intended for immediate sale. However, they are essential for the production and long-term operations of the business. Fixed assets are typically depreciated over their useful lives to account for their gradual wear and tear.

3. Investments include a company's stocks, bonds, or other securities holdings. These assets represent ownership in other companies or financial instruments. Investments can be divided into short term or long term, depending on the company's intent and ability to hold them for an extended period.

4. Intangible Assets: Intangible assets are a distinct category that includes everything that is not physical or an investment but holds significant value to the company. This category is often referred to as *intellectual capital*. Intangible assets include patents, trademarks, copyrights, brand reputations, software, customer relationships, and proprietary knowledge. These assets contribute to a company's competitive advantage and long-term success but lack a physical form.

While some researchers prefer the term *intellectual capital* instead of *intangibles*, we note that these concepts often overlap [10]. Intellectual capital covers the knowledge, skills, and other intangible assets contributing to a company's value. The distinction between these terms may depend on the specific emphasis of the research or the context in which they are used. As a subset of intangible assets, intellectual capital includes a company's knowledge, skills, and IP. It represents the intangible elements contributing to the company's value but may not be directly reflected on the balance sheet. Intellectual capital is increasingly recognized as a critical driver of innovation, competitive advantage, and overall business performance.

We may define intangibles as knowledge that can be converted into profit [11]. This viewpoint emphasizes intangibles' practical and economic utility, suggesting that their value lies in their capacity to be transformed into financial benefits for the company. We may define an intangible asset as a claim about future advantages that does not have physical or financial (a stock or a bond) embodiment [7, 9]. He adds that intangible assets generate value via innovation, unique organizational designs, or human resources practices. Intangibles often interact with tangible and financial assets to create corporate value and economic growth. This definition introduces a forward-looking aspect, highlighting that intangible assets represent potential future advantages or gains for the organization. Intangible assets lack physical existence but still hold value for the company [4]. This perspective emphasizes that the worth of intangible assets is not tied to tangible, physical properties but rather to abstract and often nonquantifiable elements, such as IP, brand reputation, or organizational know-how [6].

Similarly, the Financial Accounting Standards Board (FASB) describes intangible assets as noncurrent, nonfinancial claims to future benefits that lack physical or financial form. This definition underscores the idea that intangible assets are enduring and contribute to a company's long-term value despite not having a physical or traditional financial representation [8].

The Organization for Economic Cooperation and Development (OECD) provides a specific definition of intangible assets, describing them as something that is not a physical or financial asset. According to the OECD, intangible assets can be held in commercial activities, and the use or transfer of these assets would be reduced in a transaction between independent parties. This definition emphasizes intangible assets' nonphysical and nonfinancial nature while underlining their relevance in commercial transactions and their consideration in dealings between independent entities [5]. Expanding on this idea, intangible assets can be conceptualized as immaterial elements that serve various purposes within the business context. These assets are renewable upon consumption, meaning their utility does not diminish with use, and they can undergo changes in both quantity and quality. Unlike physical assets, intangibles have the potential for augmentation and improvement during utilization, contributing to their dynamic and evolving nature.

Thus, we may suggest that the term *intangibles* contains a range of concepts that involve knowledge, economic value, and the absence of physical form. Scholars and practitioners may use various terms interchangeably, reflecting the complexity and multidimensionality of intangible assets in the business context. These assets, including intellectual capital, IP, and other nonphysical resources, are crucial in shaping a company's competitive advantage and prospects.

Identifiable Versus Unidentifiable Intangible Assets

Intangible assets can be divided into two broad categories: identifiable and unidentifiable. Identifiable intangibles are assets with a clear identity, often legally and financially defined. They include IP, where ownership or control is discernible. The primary focus of a business is on deriving economic benefits and gauging the extent of ownership or control a firm holds over the intangible asset [2].

For an asset to be deemed identifiable, it must fulfill either of the following conditions:

a. It is separable, meaning it can be divided or separated from the entity and traded, transferred, licensed, rented, or exchanged, either on its own or alongside a related contract, identifiable asset, or liability. This holds irrespective of the entity's intention to engage in such transactions.
b. It comes from contractual or other legal rights, regardless of whether transferable or separable from the entity or other legal rights and obligations.

Goodwill, as recognized in a business combination, represents an asset embodying future economic benefits stemming from other assets acquired in the combination that are not individually identified and separately acknowledged. These future economic benefits could be attributed to synergy among the identifiable assets acquired or from assets that, on an individual basis, do not fulfill the criteria for recognition in the financial statements.

Control over an asset is established when an entity possesses the authority to derive future economic benefits from the underlying resource and can restrict others' access to those benefits. Typically, an entity's capacity to control the future economic benefits of an intangible asset is grounded in legally enforceable rights. While legal rights significantly contribute to demonstrating control, it is not an absolute prerequisite, as entities may exert control through alternative technical or organizational mechanisms. For instance, market and technical knowledge can generate future economic benefits, and an entity controls these benefits if legal protections, such as copyrights or confidentiality agreements, safeguard the knowledge. A team of skilled staff with identifiable incremental skills and anticipated ongoing contributions may also offer future economic benefits. However, such instances usually need more control to meet the criteria for defining an intangible asset [2].

Similarly, specific management or technical talent generally only meets the intangible asset definition and is protected by legal rights and fulfilling other criteria. An entity may possess a customer portfolio or market share, anticipating continued customer trading due to established relationships and loyalty. However, these items typically fall short of meeting the intangible asset definition without legal protections or alternative control mechanisms, such as evidence from exchange transactions for similar noncontractual customer relationships [2].

Furthermore, we may distinguish between entry separability and exit separability of intangible assets. Entry separability involves identifying an asset as it is produced or acquired, requiring accurate production or acquisition costs assessment. This notion aligns with accounting standards, which mandate the ascertainability of the historical cost of an intangible asset for recognition. On the other hand, exit separability implies the ability to trade the asset separately from other intangibles or the firm as a whole [1]. These issues are at the heart of the ongoing debate on intangibles. Despite certain items like goodwill, intellectual capital, human capital, organizational innovation, R&D and advertising investments, brands, and patents generally being considered intangible assets, there is little agreement in the literature regarding their precise definition, recognition, inclusion in financial statements, measurement, accounting, and depreciation [1].

What Cannot Be Considered an Intangible Asset

Tangible assets frequently intertwine with intangibles. For example, durable goods like cars or airplanes harbor patents, trademarks, and copyrights within their physical structures. Even though these intangible elements might differ from those independently developed by the firm, they contribute to the overall asset portfolio. For instance, companies like Boeing, Ford, and General Motors possess IPs, including trademarks, separate from the patents and trademarks related to their current product lineup [2].

Several economic concepts, while important, are not classified as intangible assets. It is crucial to distinguish these concepts from actual intangible assets:

1. Competitive Advantage: While a company may possess a competitive advantage, this itself is not considered an intangible asset. However, the underlying components contributing to the competitive advantage, such as manufacturing know-how or patented technologies, may qualify as intangible assets.
2. Market Share: Market share, or the portion controlled by a company, is not an intangible asset. Instead, firms acquire products or competitors that hold a specific market share.
3. Added Value: The concept of added value, which represents the additional worth a company provides to its products or services, is not considered an intangible asset. Intangible assets may contribute to added value, but the value itself is not a separate asset.
4. Efficiency: Efficiency is not a standalone intangible asset stemming from improved work processes or trade secrets. Instead, it is the outcome of specific practices or knowledge that may be classified as intangible assets.
5. Repeat Business: While desirable for companies, it is not categorized as an intangible asset. Intangible assets may contribute to customer loyalty and repeat business, but the repeat business itself is not a distinct asset.
6. Customer Loyalty: Similar to repeat business, customer loyalty is an outcome rather than an intangible asset. The factors leading to customer loyalty, such as a strong brand or unique product features, may be considered intangible assets.

It is important to note that the distinction lies in understanding that these economic concepts are outcomes or results, not standalone assets that can be bought or sold. On the other hand, intangible assets represent specific identifiable and separable elements that contribute to these economic outcomes. For instance, a firm might license its patented technologies (an intangible asset), resulting in a competitive advantage. However, the competitive advantage is not a separate asset.

Financial Assets

While financial assets lack physical substance, they carry significant economic value. Cash and cash equivalents, though not tangible, are integral financial assets. However, they do not undergo the same valuation processes as other intangibles. Cash, by definition, requires no valuation, and cash equivalents demand minimal assessment. Applying the income method to estimate the cash's future generation is impractical compared to other intangibles.

Concluding Remarks

In this chapter, we provided insights into intangible assets and some examples. The following chapter will present a typology of intangible assets, exploring various categories and types in detail.

CHAPTER 4

Typologies of Intangible Assets

Introduction

Intangible assets represent an organization's diverse array of vital resources, often neglected by conventional measures. These assets come in various forms, from those seamlessly integrated with tangible assets to those deeply intertwined within human resources. While some intangibles defy easy identification, others manifest explicitly and can be meticulously assessed through established accounting methodologies. Amidst this complexity, certain intangible assets possess the remarkable quality of being detachable from the organization, offering the potential for transfer and monetization in third-party transactions. In this chapter, we untangle the intricacies of intangible assets, identifying various typologies.

The Overlap Between Tangibles and Intangibles

Intangibles are one of three types of company assets, the other two being physical (e.g., buildings, machinery, and equipment) and financial (e.g., investments and cash). We can see, touch, taste, buy, and sell tangible assets. Anything other than tangible assets falls under the category of intangible assets. About intangibles, a common differentiation is made between identifiable and unidentifiable intangibles. Identifiable intangibles incorporate IP, including patents, copyrights, trademarks, and trade secrets. A business's primary focus should be assessing the economic benefit that can be derived and the extent of ownership or control a firm holds over the intangible asset. Although identifiable intangibles like IP typically exhibit more apparent ownership or control, this characteristic does not automatically translate into economic benefit.

While the distinction between tangible (physical) and intangible (immaterial) assets seems obvious, the two types of assets could have some intersection, implying an overlap. Tangible assets like durable goods like cars or airplanes often have associated intangibles. For example, these durable goods may contain patented technologies, making them virtual repositories of IP. Additionally, these goods carry intangibles like brands, trademarks, and copyrights, such as those found in owner's manuals. While physical assets may sometimes back financial assets, they are fundamentally intangible. Cash and cash equivalents are cited as examples of financial assets, emphasizing that they are not considered real property [2].

Types of Intangible Assets

The classification of intangible assets is a nuanced and complex issue due to the diverse definitions and perspectives surrounding them. Various researchers have proposed different categorizations, contributing to a broad spectrum of classifications. Despite the use of varied terminology, a common thread exists among many scholars who often affirm a classification into three overarching categories: human capital, customer capital, and structural capital [7]. Sullivan offers a more detailed breakdown, separating intellectual capital into three distinct categories: human capital, which is related to employees; intellectual assets, which result from human capital; and legally protected IP. These categories are interconnected, emphasizing the dynamic relationship between the different facets of intellectual capital. We may present another perspective by proposing a classification into employee competence and internal and external structures [9]. Accordingly, intangibles are fundamentally rooted in the competencies of an organization's personnel, further highlighting the role of human capital.

The American FASB takes a pragmatic approach by categorizing intangibles into technology, customer, market, workforce, contract, organization, and statutory-based assets. This classification system provides a comprehensive and tangible perspective on intangibles that is particularly relevant to financial reporting. The Schmalenbach Society in Germany introduces a detailed classification, identifying seven categories of intangibles: innovation capital, human capital, customer capital, supplier capital, investor capital, process capital, and location capital [6]. This approach offers specific examples and guidelines for distinguishing these categories, providing a more granular understanding of the various forms of intangible assets.

We may contribute to the debate by classifying intangible assets into five distinct subcategories: R&D, advertising, capital expenditures, information systems, and technology acquisition [4]. They define intangible assets as rights to future advantages devoid of physical substance, aligning with the conceptualization of intangibles as valuable rights rather than tangible entities [7].

We may classify intangible assets into three broad categories, namely (1) computerized information, (2) innovative property, and (3) economic competencies (see Table 4.1) [5]. The computerized information category includes investments that involve putting information into computers to make them useful in the long run. Examples cited are software

Table 4.1 Classification of intangible assets

Broad category	Type of investment	Type of legal property that might be created	Treated as an investment in national accounts?
Computerized information	Software development Database development	Patent, copyright, design IPR, trademark, other copyright, other	Yes, since early 2000s Recommended in SNA 1993, but OECD suggests uneven implementation
Innovative property	R&D Mineral exploration Creating entertainment and artistic originals Design and other product development costs	Patents, design IPR Patents, other Copyright, design IPR Copyright, design IPR, trademark	Yes, recommended in SNA 2008 and introduced gradually since then. Yes Yes, in EU, in the United States since 2013 No
Economic competencies	Training Market research and branding Business process reengineering	Other Copyright, trademark Patent, copyright, other	No No No

Source: [5]

(both purchased and self-developed) and databases. It notes the growing importance of big data in various industries. The innovative property category includes R&D and other product and service development forms, including design and creative endeavors. It also includes the rights associated with these innovations. The economic competencies category covers investments not directly involving innovation or computers. It involves knowledge embedded in firm-specific human and structural resources. The subcategories include marketing and branding, organizational capital, and company-specific training.

We need to bear in mind that each type of investment can generate IPR, such as patents for R&D and copyrights for entertainment investment [5]. IPR vary by country; not all investment forms can be patented in every jurisdiction. Focusing solely on patenting does not provide a complete picture of innovation metrics. Many statistical agencies now treat these spending categories as investments, but this treatment is relatively recent and can be inconsistent across countries. The recognition of database investment is noted as an example of inconsistency.

Human Capital, Structural Capital, and Relational Capital

We may split intangibles into three component classes: (1) human capital, (2) relational capital, and (3) structural capital [8].

1. Human Capital: The principal subcomponents of an organization's human capital are naturally its workforce's skillsets, know-how, depth of expertise, and breadth of experience. Human resources can be considered the living and thinking part of intangibles. Human resources include the (1) skills, knowledge, and competencies of employees and (2) know-how in specific fields that are important to the enterprise's success, plus the aptitudes and attitudes of its staff. Employee loyalty, motivation, and flexibility will often be significant factors because a firm's *expertise and experience pool* is developed over time.

2. Relational Capital: Relational capital looks at the relationships between an organization and any outside party, key individuals,

and other organizations. These include customers, intermediaries, employees, suppliers, alliance partners, regulators, pressure groups, communities, creditors, and investors. Relationships tend to fall into two categories—formalized through, for example, contractual obligations with major customers and partners, and more informal.

3. Structural Capital: Structural capital covers a broad range of vital factors. Foremost among these factors are usually the organization's essential operating processes, the way it is structured, its policies, its information flows and content of its databases, its leadership and management style, its culture, and its incentive schemes. However, it can also include legally protected intangible resources. These resources can be categorized into culture, practices, routines, and IP. Culture resources embrace corporate culture, organizational values, and management philosophies. Practices and routines can be critical organizational resources. These include internal practices, virtual networks, and review processes; these can be formal or informal procedures and tacit rules. IP—owned or legally protected intangible resources—is becoming increasingly important. Patents and trade secrets have become an essential element of competition in high-tech organizations. Here, IP is defined as the sum of resources such as patents, copyrights, trademarks, brands, registered designs, trade secrets, database content, and processes whose ownership is granted to the organization by law [8].

Identifiable Intangible Assets

Intellectual Property: The Most Important Type of Intangible Assets

When contemplating identifiable intangible assets, IP always takes center stage. The primary types of IP include patents, copyrights, trademarks, and trade secrets. A shared characteristic among IP intangibles is their historical tie to legal protection or acknowledgment. Despite being deemed property by law, there is no guarantee of the enduring economic benefits associated with these assets. Legal challenges, such as the revocation of patents, can occur, as evidenced by the high number of patent infringement lawsuits and the invalidation of patents in some cases. Another noteworthy aspect discussed is the economic marketability of IP. Owners often sell, buy, or license IP assets. This economic characteristic is particularly evident in industries like music, where song catalogs are bought and sold, and ownership can change hands over time. The ability to transfer ownership or license these assets reflects their economic value and potential revenue streams [2]. IP assets meet the criteria of being identifiable and separable. Accounting rules distinguish between tangible and intangible assets, and the separability of IP allows for their distinct identification and trade apart from the original creators or owners.

Patent

Patents, a cornerstone of IP, are regulated by over two dozen patent offices worldwide. Notable entities include the U.S. Patent and Trademark Office (USPTO), the European Patent Office, and the Japanese Patent Office. These offices collectively function as registries for IP, evaluating applications based on specific criteria. Given the digital nature of IP, issues like infringement and piracy have become more prevalent, underscoring the need for harmonizing international patent law.

The primary function of these patent offices is to serve as registries for IP. They assess whether an invention application meets specific criteria and then officially document the patentee's creation and ownership of the invention. Given the economic properties of intangible assets, there is a significant interest in safeguarding assets internationally. The ease of exchanging digital information and the digital nature of much IP have heightened concerns about infringement and piracy.

Acquiring a patent is a nontrivial task in terms of cost and duration. The surge in intangibles over recent decades has placed a substantial burden on patent offices. Typically, the process takes two to three years to secure patent approval or rejection. The application, usually crafted by a patent attorney, comprises the patent language, a review of prior art, and assurance that the application complies with legal criteria.

Patents must be "novel, non-obvious, and useful." Nonobviousness is gauged by the perspective of one with ordinary skill in the relevant art. Successful patent holders can exclude others from utilizing, making, or selling their invention for 20 years from the application filing. Various patents exist, including utility, design, plant, and animal.

The rationale behind granting patents is rooted in a straightforward economic principle: providing inventors with the ability to claim some of the profits generated by their innovations is a crucial incentive for creating those innovations. A patent is often characterized as the temporary bestowal of a monopoly. Acknowledging the efforts invested in developing a patentable idea or technology, the patent office awards the patent holder the exclusive right, for a limited period, to prevent others from using the invention outlined in the patent.

While this concept may initially appear contradictory to antitrust laws, which generally discourage the promotion of monopolies, there are broader procompetitive effects associated with granting patent protection. Consumers benefit from access to patented goods in the marketplace. Although competitors are barred from directly using the patented technology, this exclusion prevents redundant and wasteful duplication of research efforts. In theory, this avoidance of duplication contributes to more significant social benefits. It is essential to recognize that, under certain circumstances, monopolies can be advantageous for consumers. Patent law aligns with this perspective, aiming to strike the right balance of incentives by ensuring enough protection to stimulate innovation while avoiding excessive measures that might encourage misuse. The enforced expiration of patents is crucial in maintaining this delicate balance [2].

Copyright

Copyrights predominantly pertain to creative works and written materials, spanning a wide array, including books, music, photographic images, illustrations, screenplays, television and film broadcasts, and software code. In contrast to the patent application process, applying for copyright is relatively straightforward. The creator automatically holds the copyright as soon as the work is created, and filing for copyright registration serves primarily as notice of the creator's claim to the copyright. It is worth noting that while registration is a prerequisite for initiating an infringement lawsuit and holds advantages in litigation, it does not conclusively establish ownership.

A noteworthy distinction from the patent system is that individuals claiming copyright do not undergo a screening process by the copyright office for potential violations of preexisting copyrighted material. Unlike patent cases, where the willful violation is crucial, copyright law does not require willful intent for liability. When it comes to copyright, ignorance is not a defense, although it may be considered when determining damages. This highlights the nuanced nature of copyright law and the potential legal consequences, even in cases where infringement may not be intentional.

Interestingly, copyright claimants are not required to have willfully violated preexisting copyrighted works to be held liable. Unlike patents, the copyright office does not screen registrations for potential violations of existing copyrighted material.

In the digital age, the intersection of IP law and intangible assets, particularly in the concept of fair use, has become prominent. Fair use includes any use of copyrighted material that does not infringe copyright, even without authorization, provided it lacks explicit exemption under copyright law. Fair use has been historically misunderstood, and recent decades have seen significant digitalization of copyrighted material, raising new legal challenges.

Trade Secret

Trade secrets are assets from proprietary technologies or distinctive business methods, typically maintained to confer a competitive edge. Unlike one-time secrets, such as specific customer payment details on an invoice, trade secrets are ongoing elements integral to business operations, such as a unique accounting system or a closely guarded formula.

According to the Uniform Trade Secret Act (UTSA), a trade secret is defined as information, including formulas, patterns, compilations, programs, devices, methods, techniques, or processes that (1) derive independent economic value, actual or potential, from not being generally known or readily ascertainable by proper means by others who could obtain economic value from its disclosure or use and (2) are subject to reasonable efforts to maintain their secrecy. Examples of trade secrets involve a customer list, a recipe, or a factory floor layout, provided their value lies in their confidentiality and there are demonstrable efforts to keep them secret.

Unlike patents, where two firms cannot simultaneously own separate patents for the same invention, it is plausible for two firms to independently and simultaneously hold the same information as a trade secret. Essentially, owning a trade secret does not preclude the legal possibility that another entity considers the same information as its own. However, direct competition between such firms is less likely, as active competition could erode the *independent economic value* derived from the trade secret, diminishing its advantage.

Trademark

Similar to copyrights, trademarks can be established through common-law usage, but registration has distinct legal advantages. The trademark registration process occurs through the USPTO, falling somewhere between the patent and copyright processes regarding legal assistance required and the extent of review conducted.

While a trademark search is not mandatory, it is common for attorneys to conduct one to identify existing trademarks (senior marks) that might be confused with the one under consideration (junior mark). Economic analysis plays a role in determining whether two similar trademarks can coexist without confusion. Trademarks are granted for specific classes of goods, while service marks are for particular classes of services.

One crucial aspect is whether trademarks potentially overlap in customer geographies. Trademark protection can extend nationally and, in many cases, internationally. As sales and advertising via the Internet increase, the traditional geographical definition of trademarks may only sometimes suffice.

Research and Development

R&D expenditures can sometimes be recognized as identifiable intangible assets because they can lead to the creation of IP. The outcome of a firm's research efforts may translate into patents, and these patents can be bought and sold independently. It's important to note that not all R&D

expenses result in patents; however, this does not imply that the firm gains nothing in return. Marketable patents are not the sole objective of many R&D investments. Firms frequently invent and refine manufacturing techniques, software codes, and trade secrets without necessarily seeking patents for them. Conversely, firms may apply for patents without any immediate intention of commercializing the assets covered by those patents. Thus, the value derived from R&D extends beyond the acquisition of patents, containing a spectrum of innovations and improvements contributing to a firm's competitive advantage and market position.

Brands

Brands represent a convergence of trademarks, copyrights, patents, and other complex intangibles. Defining a brand is not straightforward, but at its core, it is recognized as an economic asset rather than just a label for a product. Brands extend beyond mere names or trademarks, serving as integral components of a business's assets. A renowned brand consulting firm, brands function as productive assets similar to traditional business assets like plant, equipment, cash, and investments [3]. Brands consistently delivering on their promises cultivate loyal customers, facilitating predictable cash flows and enabling confident business planning and management.

The economic benefit of brands lies in their capacity to convey information about a product, adding value to it. Consumers may associate specific attributes, such as durability, with a particular brand, making them willing to pay a premium. While a brand could exploit its reputation in the short term by cutting corners, the market would eventually uncover any deception, leading to a loss of consumer trust and a diminished willingness to pay a premium.

Naming rights, an extension of a brand, are exemplified by domain and building names. Companies seek to associate their Internet addresses with their brand names, with the value of a particular domain name not yet established. Naming rights also extend to uniform resource locators (URLs), motivated by a company's concern about inappropriate use of similar Web addresses affecting its brand. Courts have generally favored companies over cybersquatters who attempt to profit from registering domain names of popular companies.

Software Codes

Software code stands out as one of the most complex forms of IP to delineate, as it can be copyrighted, the business process enabled by the code can be patented, parts of the code can be maintained as trade secrets, and features of the software design can be trademarked. Firms invest substantial proportions of their intellectual capital, often dominating their overall investments, in software development. The accounting treatment for software depends on whether it serves as an input to manufacturing a firm's product or if the software itself is the primary product and the degree of proprietary nature associated with the software investment.

Firms' utilization and sale of software code can vary significantly, reflecting different accounting treatments. This divergence is influenced by whether the software is a component used in manufacturing the firm's goods or if the software is the core product itself. Additionally, the accounting treatment is influenced by the software investment's level of proprietary protection.

To illustrate, many law firms invest substantially in software applications for various purposes, such as Microsoft Office for Word processing and spreadsheet calculations, Intuit's QuickBooks for bookkeeping, and Thomson's Westlaw for online legal research. However, these software investments may not qualify as valuable intangible property for law firms. Using widely available software like Microsoft Office, QuickBooks, and Westlaw does not confer a competitive advantage to one law firm over another because many firms use similar programs. Nonetheless, these software products are precious intangible property for creators like Microsoft and Intuit.

Unidentifiable Intangible Assets

Unidentifiable intangible assets, equally significant as their identifiable counterparts, are assets within a firm that remain undisclosed in accounting terms until an event, such as an acquisition or merger, brings them to light. Among these, goodwill is the most frequently referenced unidentifiable intangible asset, typically from firm-specific capital.

Goodwill

In accounting terms, goodwill carries a distinct meaning beyond the common notions of customer loyalty, satisfaction, repeat business, or positive relationships. These outcomes are typically attributed to other assets, whether tangible or intangible, such as superior products or better services. Financial accountants define goodwill as a residual element, emerging when one firm acquires another for an amount exceeding the fair value of the net identifiable assets, including both tangible and intangible assets.

While there are other unidentifiable intangibles, traditional accounting principles offer limited guidance on their measurement; an example of such an intangible could be an efficiently organized factory floor. If the efficiency can be patented, it becomes identifiable; however, often, the efficiency remains unspecified or deliberately kept as a trade secret. In the event of a sale, the value of such efficiency might be categorized under goodwill.

Customer lists, though identifiable, are often cited as contributing to the excess fair market value in an acquisition, generating goodwill. Precision is required to accurately attribute value to a customer list to understand how it adds value. For instance, the list format in an electronic database can be valuable for a company with a large customer base. Organized customer information, including location, contact details, and purchased product models, can be crucial for various purposes, such as warranty business.

Alternatively, customer lists represent the long-term expected sales revenue from existing and potential customers. This perspective assumes that the lists indicate repeat business or promising leads. However, it is essential to recognize that the ultimate source of repeat or new business lies in desirable product attributes or other services provided by the company. These features may constitute the unidentifiable intangibles that hold significance for measuring future revenues. Thus, a customer list, on its own, may not hold substantial meaning, as the actual value lies in the company's ability to deliver desirable product offerings that secure future revenues.

Human Capital and Organizational Capital

Gary Becker (1964 [1985]) and other influential economists established the economic concept of human capital, distinguishing it from financial or physical assets by emphasizing that human capital cannot be separated from the individuals who possess it [1]. Human capital includes both physical and intellectual abilities, including investments in education, training, medical care, and other factors that enhance health, earnings, and personal development over an individual's lifetime.

Following Becker's introduction of the concept, economists and consultants began subdividing and classifying types of human capital [1]. Terms like *intellectual capital, organizational capital,* and *knowledge capital* are often used interchangeably. However, the distinctions between them may not always be clear.

Organizational capital refers to capital that resides within an organization. However, it is crucial to distinguish ownership within the organization. Some organizational capital arises from the specific arrangement of a firm's assets. At the same time, other forms reside within the firm, such as the education levels of its employees. We may distinguish firm-specific creations as organizational capital. Such capital remains with the firm even when employees leave, primarily if it is codified in patents, copyrights, or trade secrets.

Another form of organizational capital is more temporal, representing shared knowledge or efficiencies from employees working together. For example, a long-term collaboration between an attorney and her legal assistant may create efficient work processes. However, these efficiencies may not be transferable when employees go home, and the firm might lose these benefits if the team is separated. Valuing such *gray area* organizational capital poses challenges, as these assets are often concealed and difficult to assess regarding ownership.

Concluding Remarks

In this chapter, we provided a breakdown of the various typologies of intangible assets, examining their diverse categories and characteristics.

In the next chapter, we will analyze the distinctive features of intangible assets.

CHAPTER 5

The Distinctive Features of Intangibles

Introduction

Despite their diversity, intangible assets share several distinctive features that set them apart from tangible assets. Nonscarcity, nonrivalry, limited tradability, high scalability, low or zero marginal costs, network effects, synergies, spillover effects, and partial excludability are some important distinctive features of intangible assets (see Table 5.1). The following chapter examines the intangible assets' unique features, analyzing their implications and significance in business and management.

Knowledge Content

Intangible assets are often identified by their core component of knowledge, a crucial aspect recognized in various intangible categories [3, 7]. When looked at from a neo-classical perspective, companies engage in collaborative efforts primarily to spread the risks associated with creating technological knowledge. We may identify three key characteristics of knowledge: firstly, knowledge is considered a public good, making it unsuitable for traditional market dynamics because producers cannot fully control its use; secondly, creating knowledge is inherently uncertain; and thirdly, there are economies of scale in knowledge production [1]. Intangible assets inherently possess all three of these characteristics. When knowledge is viewed as a public good, its accessibility is not limited. Once created, it can be shared and used by various entities without being depleted. However, this characteristic poses a challenge for knowledge producers in capturing the total economic value of their work because there is no built-in exclusivity in its use. The inherent uncertainty in knowledge

Table 5.1 The distinctive features of intangible assets

Feature	Description	Examples/implications
Knowledge content	Intangibles contain explicit or implicit information	Knowledge: Is unsuitable for conventional markets It cannot be fully appropriated Is a public good Its creation is uncertain Involves economies of scale
Nonscarcity (Nonrivalry)	Intangibles are not scarce, and their opportunity costs are minimal	Intangibles are immaterial and almost unlimited
Limited tradability	Intangibles lack organized and active markets	They involve: High transaction costs Informal contacts and transactions Trust and relationships
Risk and information asymmetries	Intangibles are uncertain and nebulous	Uncertain financial performance Fear of imitation
High scalability	Intangibles can be produced in mass	They can be scaled almost infinitely
Low or zero marginal cost	Intangibles are cheap to reproduce	They do not involve the significant cost of reproduction
High initial investment	Intangibles require significant initial investment	Barriers to entry are significant
Network effects	Intangibles gain value after application	The networks of Uber drivers, Airbnb hosts, and Instagram users gain value after use
Sunken costs	Intangibles cannot be recovered if decisions are reversed	Intangible assets are difficult to sell and are often specific to the firm that owns them
Spillovers	One company's intangibles benefit other businesses	Intangibles are nonrivalrous, nonexcludable, fluid
Synergies	Existing intangibles create new and more valuable intangibles	The effects of intangibles are compounded as they are combined, making them more valuable than individual assets
Partial excludability (contested ownership)	Intangible ownership is less protected	Firms struggle to internalize intangibles through effective strategies
Shared/multiple consumption	They can be shared and concurrently utilized by multiple consumers	Justifies business approaches like franchising or licensing Businesses may tap into diverse audiences simultaneously
Environmental sustainability	Intangible assets do not significantly contribute to the depletion of finite natural resources	Intangibles minimize the need for physical resources and contribute to the environment conservation

creation means that predicting the outcome of knowledge generation is tricky. Unlike tangible assets with more predictable outcomes, creating knowledge involves unpredictability and variability, introducing an element of risk into investing in intangible assets. Additionally, economies of scale in knowledge production indicate that the cost per unit decreases as the volume of knowledge produced increases. This aligns with the idea that more collaborative efforts or investments in knowledge creation can lead to more efficient and cost-effective outcomes, underscoring the collective nature of knowledge development.

Nonscarcity (Nonrivalry)

Physical, human, and financial assets face rivalry and struggle [6]. By contrast, intangible assets exhibit nonrivalry and minimal opportunity costs. This unique characteristic stems primarily from the inherent nature of intangible assets, distinguished by substantial fixed (sunk) costs and marginal costs that are typically negligible or zero. Intangible assets are costly to create initially but relatively inexpensive to reproduce [2]. The substantial fixed costs associated with intangible asset creation denote the investments required upfront. Once developed, however, these assets often incur minimal additional costs for reproduction. This cost structure contributes to the nonrivalrous nature of intangible assets, as their reproduction does not incur the same expenses as the initial creation. In practical terms, this characteristic influences firms' strategic decisions regarding the control and management of intangible assets. Given the potential for simultaneous global utilization of these assets, companies frequently choose to centralize control and management at single headquarters. The centralization allows for efficient coordination, ensuring optimal use of intangible assets across diverse markets without redundant investments in separate management structures.

The notion of nonrivalry in intangible assets implies that using these assets does not diminish their availability for others. Unlike physical or human resources, where one entity's utilization may limit access to others, multiple entities can employ intangible assets without significant competition or depletion.

Limited Tradability

Determining legal ownership of intangible assets poses a more elusive challenge compared to tangible assets, and even the existence of IPR does not always provide clear boundaries for the appropriation of such assets. Despite these complexities, it is noteworthy that intangible asset markets do exist [6]. However, what sets intangibles apart is the absence of organized and active marketplaces featuring numerous participants and transparent pricing mechanisms, a characteristic that distinguishes them from other asset classes. The lack of well-defined markets for intangible assets does not mean they are excluded from economic exchange; their transactions take a distinctive form. The high transaction costs associated with intangibles necessitate a departure from traditional market structures. Instead, exchanges involving intangible assets often occur through informal contacts facilitated by frequent interactions and a foundation of trust between parties. This informal mode of exchange acknowledges the challenges in establishing formal marketplaces and the need for a nuanced approach to intangible asset transactions. The limited tradability of intangibles aligns with classical literature that confirms the imperfections of a free market when dealing with knowledge and information [1, 8].

In part, failures in establishing organized markets for intangibles can be attributed to the inherent difficulty in crafting comprehensive contracts that adequately address the nuanced outcomes associated with intangible assets [9].

Risk and Information Asymmetries

Creating intangible assets through education, R&D, and innovation is notably associated with uncertainty. The transmission of intangibles, safeguarded by property rights, introduces a heightened level of risk, primarily due to the inherent information asymmetry associated with these assets. Challenges in identifying and quantifying intangibles give rise to principal–agent conflicts among the parties engaged in exchanging such assets. Moreover, managing intangible assets proves to be an exceptionally uncertain process, often akin to navigating in the dark [6]. The knowledge-intensive nature of most intangibles contributes to the risk factor. Predicting outputs from nonphysical inputs becomes challenging, making it difficult for firms to capture returns from essentially intangible assets [5]. The commercial innovation risk is further compounded by the fear of imitation, which can limit the returns an innovator obtains from their creative efforts.

While intangible assets have the potential for future economic benefits, such as revenue generation, cost savings, or advantages derived from their application, recognizing and measuring these assets necessitates specific criteria. These criteria include assessing the probability of expected future economic benefits flowing to the entity and ensuring the reliable measurement of the asset's cost. Managerial judgment plays a crucial role in evaluating the degree of certainty associated with the anticipated flow of future economic benefits.

High Scalability

Intangible assets possess a distinctive characteristic known as scalability, setting them apart from physical assets. This means that intangible assets can be utilized repeatedly and simultaneously across multiple locations or instances with minimal additional cost once created or acquired. Examples of scalable intangible assets include operating manuals, software applications, and product designs for jet engines. Scalability often encourages more firms to enter markets, potentially leading to industry concentration dominated by a few large companies. In markets where assets are highly scalable, a winner-takes-all dynamic often emerges, making it challenging for competitors to establish a significant presence. Unlike physical assets that degrade and wear out over time, certain intangible assets, such as Google's data and algorithms or Coca-Cola's brand, can scale without diminishing value. This resilience contributes to these assets' enduring significance and value in an evolving economic environment. In the intangible economy, where costs do not rise directly in proportion to revenues, businesses strive to achieve scale and maximize revenue. Creating truly differentiated intangible assets becomes crucial in ensuring that the revenue generated from scale effectively manages costs. This emphasis on differentiation highlights the importance of developing unique and valuable intangible assets that set a business apart from its competitors, contributing to sustained success and competitiveness in the market.

Low or Zero Marginal Cost

Low or zero marginal cost refers to the phenomenon where the cost of producing each additional product unit becomes negligible or approaches zero. This concept particularly applies to intangible products, where the initial creation of the asset incurs a significant investment. However, the cost of duplicating or distributing additional units is minimal. Examples of intangible products with zero or near-zero marginal cost include digital media, software, online educational materials, e-books, apps, music, electronic artwork, and information in general. For example, once a song, movie, or book is created digitally, making additional copies for distribution incurs minimal cost. Online platforms, streaming services, and e-book stores can replicate and deliver these products to unlimited users without significant additional expenses. Software applications, especially those distributed digitally, often have zero marginal cost. Once the initial development is complete, making copies for users or distributing updates involves negligible expenses. Open-source software, in particular, can be freely duplicated and shared. Like software, mobile applications have low marginal costs once the development is finished. App developers can distribute their creations to millions of users through app stores without incurring substantial costs for each download. Once data or information is collected and organized, the cost of providing access or distributing that information to additional users is minimal. This applies to databases, research reports, and various informational products.

High Initial Investment

The characteristic of high initial investment in intangibles is marked by substantial costs incurred during the early stages of creating IP. This feature is evident across diverse industries, including pharmaceuticals, software development, and entertainment. It reflects the significant financial commitment required before realizing tangible economic benefits.

Pharmaceutical companies invest substantial sums in their product pipeline, including research, development, and clinical trials. The costs are incurred well before the possibility of commercialization, covering the extensive efforts to discover, test, and secure regulatory approvals for new drugs. This high initial investment is a calculated risk, with the expectation that successful drugs will offset the costs associated with unsuccessful ones. Software firms allocate considerable resources in terms of person-hours and financial investments to create new software products. Even seemingly simple programming features can demand several thousand hours of testing and development. The iterative nature of software development involves continuous refinement, contributing to the high initial costs before a product is ready for release. Movie and television studios face substantial expenses in producing content, covering script development, casting, filming, postproduction, and marketing. While blockbuster hits like Titanic and Harry Potter yield significant returns, the average revenue for films can be considerably lower than the production costs. The industry adopts a portfolio approach, where successful projects aim to compensate for less profitable or unsuccessful ones.

In creative fields, such as songwriting and inventions, the apparent simplicity of a successful creation often opposes years of experimentation and investment. The initial investment includes the costs of failed attempts, low-pay periods, and the acquisition of skills and knowledge that contribute to the eventual successful creation. The infrequent big successes support the more frequent small losses, forming a portfolio strategy for managing the inherent risks of creative endeavors. The notion of a portfolio is central to how industries view their intangible assets. It acknowledges that not every creative endeavor or innovative project will yield significant financial returns. Instead, the successes are expected to outweigh the costs associated with the numerous attempts, creating a sustainable and profitable overall intellectual property portfolio.

Network Affects

Network effects manifest when the value of a particular asset rises proportionally to the increasing number of users engaging with it. This phenomenon is inherently rooted in demand-side dynamics, with intangible assets often deriving value from synergies with other intangibles, thus generating self-reinforcing loops. Platforms are prime examples of intangible value creators, showcasing this concept by drawing in users who contribute more data and superior algorithms. This, in turn, enhances the platform's overall appeal, creating a cycle that attracts new customers and partners [4]. Notable examples include the networks of Uber drivers, Airbnb hosts, and Instagram users, along with the foundational standards of the World Wide Web.

The positive feedback loop generated by network effects amplifies the utility or value of an asset as its user base expands. However, it is crucial to note that network effects are not universally positive and can give rise to congestion issues, particularly in technologies such as high-speed cable Internet broadband services. The influx of additional users may negatively impact access speed for existing users. It is imperative to distinguish network effects from economies of scale, as the latter pertains to supply-side advantages leading to cost savings with increased production scale. By contrast, network effects emanate from heightened demand and a growing user base, exerting an influence on the utility or value of the asset.

Sunken Costs

Sunken costs represent investments that cannot be quickly recovered if a business reverses a decision. Recouping costs associated with intangible assets poses a more significant challenge than tangible assets. Unlike tangible assets such as machinery and vehicles, which can be relatively quickly sold in the event of bankruptcy, intangible assets like brand reputation and operational procedures present a more difficult hurdle for liquidation. This complexity arises from the fact that intangible assets are often tied to a company's unique identity, making them less attractive to potential buyers. Unlike tangible assets that can be mass-produced and standardized, intangible assets are frequently bespoke and tailored to the specific needs of the company that owns them. This specificity renders them less interchangeable between businesses and diminishes their marketability. The sale of intangible assets, such as knowledge and know-how, further complicates the requirement for formal IPR for protection. Intangible assets may lack active buyers; even when they do, the transaction process is often complicated and demanding.

The challenges associated with recovering intangible assets are exacerbated by their company-specific nature. Many intangible assets are closely aligned with the distinctiveness of the firm that possesses them, rendering them less valuable or relevant to other entities. This uniqueness not only limits their potential market but also adds complexity to the sale process, making it a less straightforward endeavor than tangible assets.

Spillovers

Spillovers refer to scenarios in which the intangible investments of one company inadvertently confer benefits upon other businesses, often without the original company's deliberate intent. A quintessential illustration of intangible assets characterized by substantial spillover effects is R&D investments. R&D endeavors generate nonrivalrous ideas, meaning that using the idea does not deplete its availability to others, and it is nonexcludable, implying that it is challenging to prevent others from utilizing the idea unless legally protected.

The domains where spillovers are prominent include product design, marketing strategies, organizational innovation, and employee training. These spillover effects materialize when the investments made by one company exert an influential or inspiring impact on other firms within the same industry, creating a ripple effect of knowledge diffusion and innovation.

In contrast to the well-established laws and norms governing the ownership of physical assets that have evolved over thousands of years, the legal framework and norms surrounding intangible asset ownership are relatively recent. This nascent stage in developing intangible asset ownership laws makes them more contested and uncertain, introducing complexities and challenges to determining the rightful ownership and protection of intangible assets.

The dynamic nature of spillovers of intangible investments highlights the complex interplay between companies within an industry. As intangible assets become increasingly pivotal in the contemporary business environment, navigating the evolving ownership laws and norms becomes essential for companies seeking to harness the benefits of spillovers while addressing the challenges associated with the ambiguous nature of intangible asset ownership.

Synergies

Synergies refer to the strategic amalgamation of existing ideas and innovations to give rise to novel technologies and products. The process of technological advancement frequently hinges on the integration and synthesis of preexisting ideas and technologies. The evolution of ideas follows a dynamic pattern of exchange, wherein the combination of different concepts and technologies catalyzes the generation of new and more valuable innovations, resulting in a pyramid of progressive advancements. The root of this phenomenon lies in the recognition that the true potential of innovations is unleashed when diverse ideas converge. The synergy achieved by combining these disparate elements transcends the sum of individual assets, thereby amplifying their overall value. This interconnected web of ideas indicates the collaborative nature of technological progress. It confirms how the convergence of varied concepts fuels innovation. Notably, synergies between intangible assets possess an intriguing quality of unpredictability, often transcending traditional domain boundaries. These synergies' cross-domain nature adds dynamism and complexity to the innovation environment, as breakthroughs can emerge from unexpected intersections of knowledge and expertise.

Moreover, the interplay between intangible and tangible assets in technological innovation is pivotal. Information technologies, exemplified by computers and smartphones, showcase the dance between intangible investments and tangible assets. The harmonious integration of software, algorithms, and user interfaces, which are intangible, with the physical hardware of computers and smartphones exemplifies the symbiotic relationship between these asset categories, emphasizing the holistic approach necessary for technological advancements.

The concept of synergies implies the collaborative and iterative nature of innovation, illustrating that the whole is often more significant than the sum of its parts. Recognizing and harnessing synergies as industries evolve becomes paramount for organizations aiming to stay at the forefront of technological progress.

Partial Excludability (Contested Ownership)

While the ownership of specific intangibles, such as a company's brands or various forms of intellectual capital, enjoys well-established legal recognition and protection, the ownership status of other intangibles, particularly a firm's labor force and human capital, is comparatively less secure. Moreover, certain intangible assets, like a customer base, exist outside the firm's legal confines, posing challenges in establishing exclusive ownership. Persistent ownership dilemmas persist despite companies' endeavors to internalize these valuable sources through strategies to foster enduring connections between employees and consumers [3]. For example, investments in the training and development of employees, though beneficial for the firm, create a scenario where the advantages of a skilled workforce extend beyond the organization itself. Trained employees, upon changing jobs, carry their enhanced skills and knowledge to other companies, thereby contributing to the broader societal benefit [3, 6]. In intangible asset management, informal and formal institutions play a pivotal role in deriving value from stored intangible assets by enforcing excludability. In managing intangible assets, excludability is often formalized and upheld through legal systems, incorporating mechanisms such as patents, copyrights, and noncompete clauses.

Shared/Multiple Consumption

Intangible assets possess a distinct quality of shareability, allowing them to be concurrently utilized by multiple consumers. This characteristic finds suitable illustration in events like musical concerts or sports gatherings, where the experience is available to thousands of spectators in the physical venue. It simultaneously reaches millions of viewers through television and Internet broadcasts. This feature, simultaneous consumption, holds considerable strategic significance, justifying business approaches like franchising or licensing. About simultaneous consumption, businesses leverage the expansive reach of intangible assets to tap into diverse audiences simultaneously. For instance, a sports franchise may franchise its brand or license its events, enabling multiple entities to capitalize on the shared experience offered by the sporting events. This approach broadens the audience base and creates avenues for revenue generation by making the intangible asset accessible to a wide range of consumers. Recognizing the simultaneous consumption feature becomes a cornerstone for business strategies aimed at rapid growth. Franchising, for example, allows businesses to extend their reach by allowing third-party operators to rep-licate their successful models. On the other hand, licensing enables busi-nesses to grant others the right to use specific elements of their intangible assets, expanding the asset's impact across various markets.

Environmental Sustainability

The transition to an intangible economy strongly aligns with sustain-ability principles, as intangible assets do not significantly contribute to the depletion of finite natural resources. Unlike their tangible counter-parts, which often require raw materials and contribute to environmental degradation through resource extraction and manufacturing processes, intangible assets, characterized by their nonmaterial nature, reduce their ecological footprint. The shift toward digitization, especially in industries where physical testing and prototyping are essential, enhances efficiency and contributes to environmental conservation. Simulating complex pro-cedures like aircraft engine tests through digital platforms minimizes the need for physical prototypes. This reduction in physical testing conserves resources and significantly curtails greenhouse gas emissions associated with traditional manufacturing and testing processes. By leveraging the power of information processes over physical ones, industries within the intangible economy demonstrate a forward-thinking approach that enhances efficiency and innovation and actively mitigates environmental impact, promoting a more sustainable and ecologically responsible busi-ness paradigm.

Concluding Remarks

This chapter offered insights into the distinctive features of intangible assets. As we will see in the next five chapters, due to these features intan-gible assets bring about significant implications for different functions of business including management, strategy, finance and accounting, invest-ment, marketing, and consumption.

PART 2

Managing in Intangible Capitalism

CHAPTER 6

Organization and Management

Introduction

Intangible assets have profound implications for how businesses are managed and organized. In this chapter, we will examine these implications, exploring how they affect everything from how organizations are structured to how supply chains are managed. Additionally, we will investigate how intangible assets influence the roles of managers and workers and the overall organization of work within companies. By dissecting these aspects, we aim to understand better the far-reaching impact intangible assets have on modern business operations.

Shifts in the Organizational Structure of Corporations

The emergence of the intangible economy has been linked to the reorganization transformation of large multinational companies during the 1990s. This evolution marked a departure from the conventional multidivisional structures to embrace more dynamic and adaptable forms, notably the segmented and network forms. This paradigm shift was particularly notable in the computer, communications, and automotive sectors [1]. The segmented form, a manifestation of this organizational shift, is characterized by a heightened level of autonomy granted to individual divisions. Strategic decision making is decentralized, fostering a more agile response to the rapid evolution of new product or process innovations.

Building on this decentralization, the network form takes organizational flexibility further. It points out the significance of autonomy among divisions. It emphasizes multidirectional and intensive communication, both internally within the firm and externally. At different organizational levels—be it corporate, work, or product development—divisions and workers are entrusted with a degree of autonomy. Horizontal communication becomes pivotal for ensuring effective coordination and in a rapidly changing market. This decentralization and the adoption of network structures are driven by the imperative to swiftly respond to shifts in consumer tastes and market dynamics, significantly as product life cycles shorten and innovation accelerates relentlessly. Central to this organizational evolution is the recognition that networks are pivotal in managing intangible assets, particularly in nurturing relationships with suppliers and competitors for collaborative R&D and product development. Companies increasingly embrace outsourcing for specific activities and form robust supplier networks to concentrate on their core competencies, resulting in efficiency gains and heightened innovation capabilities.

Consequently, a firm's competitiveness is no longer solely defined by the ownership of tangible assets; instead, it hinges significantly on its capacity to manage networks effectively [1]. The transformation toward decentralized and network-centric structures is a strategic response to the evolving environment of the intangible economy. Effectively navigating and leveraging networks has become crucial for large firms aiming to uphold and improve their competitiveness in an environment where intangible assets and dynamic collaboration are paramount.

Changing and Challenging the Roles of Managers

Intangible assets display synergies and spillover effects, necessitating skillful management through internal coordination and external networks. In the contemporary environment of intangible capitalism, power distribution has undergone a significant transformation. Unlike the past, where ownership of a firm's resources rested predominantly with shareholders or owners, today's intangible economy sees resources distributed among diverse stakeholders, including employees, the local community, suppliers, competitors, government bodies, and customers. Consequently, market power determinants are no longer anchored in factors like cost or scale but rather in the proficiency to supervise these complex networks effectively. This paradigm shift is evident in prominent companies such as Microsoft, Gucci, LVMH, and even automotive manufacturers [1]. At the managerial level, the governance challenge has evolved from ensuring that employees act in the company's best interests to proficiently managing internal and external networks. In times when a firm's value was primarily linked to tangible assets susceptible to ownership, the firm's boundaries were relatively fixed, and concerns about integrity were minimal. By contrast, in today's business landscape, the central management challenge is to connect the owners of intangible assets to the firm's activities by providing them access to some resources without relinquishing excessive control, as this could compromise the overall integrity of the firm [9]. Effectively handling a network has become a pivotal challenge, as it contributes to creating successful products and services, turning a well-managed network into a valuable intangible asset that is difficult for competitors to replicate. These networks involve heightened communication, autonomy, and collaboration across different divisions, resembling assets in their own right. These networks extend within and outside the firm, fostering relationships with suppliers and competitors, particularly in R&D and product development [1].

Given these complex challenges in an intangible-intensive economy, there is a premium on managers capable of skillfully managing internal synergies and external networks [7]. Managers and leaders assume celebrity status in the new intangible capitalism, receiving substantial rewards and recognition [7]. The fundamental attribution error has elevated managers to revered figures, prompting boards of directors to grant them high salaries and rewards under the assumption that managers are solely responsible for the company's success.

Doing More With Less

Traditionally, a company's power was closely tied to its revenue, market capitalization, physical assets, and the size of its workforce. Robust revenues were typically associated with large employee numbers and significant physical holdings. However, the conditions have undergone a profound shift in the last three decades, marked by the dominance of intangible capitalism [4]. In this new era, prominent businesses have achieved heightened revenues with fewer employees and reduced physical assets. According to the International Monetary Fund (IMF), labor income shares began trending down in advanced economies in the 1980s.

They reached their lowest level in the past half-century, just before the global financial crisis 2008 [8].

Current corporations are redefining conventional norms, showcasing a paradigm where sizable revenues and profits coexist with modest physical assets and a streamlined workforce. For instance, in 2023, Meta (Facebook), with a workforce of 66,000, generated an impressive U.S.$126.95 billion in revenues and held a market capitalization of U.S.$909.62 billion. Similarly, with a market capitalization exceeding U.S.$180 billion and revenues nearing U.S.$32.743 billion in 2023, Netflix maintained a remarkably lean workforce of 12,800 employees. Such examples extend beyond information technology, as advancements in automation, global production, branding, and outsourcing empower major corporations to enhance productivity, achieving more significant revenues with fewer employees and reduced physical assets. In 2022, sectors like software and investment banking exhibited averages of U.S.$4.5 million and U.S.$2 million in market capitalization per employee, coupled with U.S.$1.2 million and U.S.$1 million in revenues per employee, respectively. This trend highlights a departure from the traditional correlation between workforce size and financial metrics. Prominent multinational corporations (MNCs) like Nike, Apple, Vizio, ExxonMobil, and AT&T exemplify this paradigm shift by increasing productivity while trimming their workforce. Even in the oil industry, ExxonMobil, a global powerhouse, has significantly reduced its workforce from 150,000 in the 1960s to less than 75,000 despite merging with a challenging rival [5]. This strategic restructuring reflects the broader trend wherein companies leverage automation, global networks, brand strength, and outsourcing to optimize productivity, generating substantial revenues and market valuations with a leaner workforce and fewer tangible assets. Thus, we may suggest that in contemporary intangible capitalism, traditional metrics are obsolete, and a company's size in terms of physical assets and employees is no longer the sole determinant of its financial success.

Supply Chain Management in Intangible Economy

The rise of intangible capitalism is tied to the recent surge in the expansion of global value chains over the last three decades. The first wave of industrialization, triggered by the steam engine in the 18th century, primarily dealt with the exchange of commodities and fully assembled manufactured goods. However, the subsequent wave of globalization witnessed a pronounced shift toward heightened vertical specialization. During this second wave, countries began focusing on specific production stages, giving rise to multidirectional trade in intermediate goods and services within specific industries. This shift marked a significant increase in the reliance on intangible assets. Factors such as lower transport costs, advancements in transportation and telecommunication, and the liberalization of trade policies played pivotal roles in the formation of complex global value chains [8].

A historical perspective reveals that the early 1900s, characterized by Ford's introduction of mass production, emphasized transforming raw materials into final products within a limited number of stages, typically within the same factory or vicinity. Fast forward to the 21st century, and the manufacturing process is often represented by a *smile curve*. Coined by the CEO of Acer in the early 1990s, this curve illustrates that more value is added in stages preceding and following actual manufacturing. These stages correspond to manipulating intangible assets, including R&D, design, branding, and after-sales services [3].

Companies navigating this setting face two primary questions: firstly, whether to handle various production tasks internally or delegate them to other entities, and secondly, where these tasks should be executed. Economic theory suggests that firms outsource specific production tasks when market costs exceed internal coordination costs. However, companies are more likely to integrate tasks when strong synergies exist, such as combining product development and manufacturing. Concerns about technology leakage to competitors may also drive vertical integration. Nevertheless, factors like increased production complexity, the growing importance of pre- and postmanufacturing stages, the standardization of specific manufacturing processes, and advancements in information and communication technologies have favored greater specialization over time.

Vertical specialization can occur within firms or across them. Companies may offshore manufacturing by establishing subsidiaries in foreign countries or outsourcing offshore manufacturing to independent firms.

The specific configuration of global value chains, including the number of firms involved and their relationships, varies significantly across industries. Academic research distinguishes between buyer-driven and producer-driven chains. In buyer-driven chains, large retailers and branded merchandisers set production and quality standards for independent suppliers. By contrast, in supplier-driven chains, leading firms possess advanced technological capabilities and rely on independent suppliers for specialized inputs.

Generating new knowledge introduces a tradeoff for firms, deciding between keeping innovations secret for a competitive edge or opting for IP rights, which require disclosure but offer exclusivity for a limited time. This decision hinges on factors such as the nature of the knowledge asset and whether it can be easily kept secret. Additionally, IPR may not extend to all types of knowledge assets. Specialized workers' skills also constitute crucial knowledge assets for a company's strategy. Retaining these skills is essential, but legal constraints, such as noncompete clauses in employment contracts, impose limits. In the intangible economy, global value chain configurations are influenced by knowledge management considerations, guiding firms in deciding whether to integrate production tasks or outsource them. Outsourcing involves cost savings but also poses risks of knowledge leakage. Effective knowledge management strategies, including securing IPR, are pivotal in mitigating these risks.

Firms may choose to openly share or license knowledge assets to encourage technology adoption and gain access to others' technology. IP protection, particularly patents, is critical to a firm's knowledge management strategy. Obtaining patents can be costly, leading companies to limit coverage to countries with significant economic importance and involvement in global value chain production. Reputational assets, similar to knowledge assets, also influence the organization of global value chains. Outsourcing parts of the production process may expose lead firms to reputational risks if the quality of inputs is compromised. Trademarks and geographical indications (GIs) are crucial IP instruments protecting reputational assets. Managing a global portfolio of trademarks requires strategic decision making, covering various aspects beyond product names, such as shapes, sounds, and associated colors.

The Fluidity of the Organization of Work

The advent of the intangible economy and the integration of information technologies have prompted a profound restructuring of companies within global networks, transcending traditional spatial and temporal constraints [15]. In this transformative setting, intangible assets have diminished the imperative for physical presence, enabling corporations to reach customers remotely. Simultaneously, there has been a notable shift from rigid and stable organizational structures toward more flexible, project-oriented modes of operation [6]. Many companies have embraced the technological infrastructure to transition their operations remotely. Consequently, the workplace in the intangible economy has morphed into a virtual area or a *nonspace*, where spatial, social, and local institutional constraints are either eliminated or weakened. This shift implies a tempo-spatial compression, wherein the world is experienced socially and materially as a smaller place [10,12].

The evolving organizational forms now center around electronically connected networks of contractors, freelancers, and semiautonomous entities [11, 14, 15, 16]. This transition means a gradual shift in work focus from stable organizational structures to flexible and project-based operations. Employers increasingly turn to part-time, contingent, and contract workers to meet business goals.

The evolving concept of the workplace gradually renders geographic locations less relevant, challenging the significance of cities as economic activity centers. Work-from-home arrangements offer high degrees of flexibility and are highly valued by a majority of workers. Simultaneously, organizations recognize that remote work provides multiple advantages, including lower overhead expenses, heightened managerial control, robust information systems, and expedited digital decision making. Despite ongoing technological transformations, maximizing efficiency and productivity from office space and stringent control over associated costs remain a top priority for employers [13]. However, the fluidity in work arrangements does not equate to unlimited employee freedom, as employers increasingly rely on new data-driven tools to monitor and control offsite workers. Additionally, as organizations transition to telework and remote business, new challenges associated with distance management surface, making skills in managing uncertainty and facilitating global work more critical [2].

Employers' growing reliance on part-time, contingent, contractual, and specialized workers represents a departure from the traditional workplace model. This shift highlights the dynamic nature of the contemporary work environment and the need for adaptive structures to navigate the complexities of the intangible economy.

Concluding Remarks

This chapter sheds light on some salient organizational, management, work, and supply chain features in the new intangible capitalism. In the next chapter, we will examine the evolving strategy and competitiveness in the era of the intangible economy.

CHAPTER 7

Strategic and Competitive Considerations

Introduction

In this chapter, our attention is directed toward crucial aspects of firm strategy and competitiveness. We examine the transformative impact of intangible assets on corporate balance sheets, reshaping the fundamental landscape of strategic management. The emergence of intangible assets introduces a notable divergence between industry frontrunners and stragglers, consequently fostering an environment where the winners take it all. Moreover, our exploration extends to scrutinizing the intricate interplay between the ascent of intangible assets, firms' clustering, and the dynamics of firms' competitive positioning.

Shift in Strategy and Competitiveness

The rise of intangible capitalism necessitates reevaluating competitive strategies as the differentiation among firms increasingly relies on intangible elements such as proprietary processes, brands, robust relationships, and knowledge capital. Unlike a few decades ago, when physical and financial assets dominated, modern competitiveness places intangible assets at the forefront of value creation. These intangible assets are the primary source of sustainable competitive advantage due to their rarity, inimitability, and nonsubstitutability [16, 18]. In the intangible economy, the ownership and strategic control of valuable IP and data emerge as pivotal drivers of economic prosperity. The ability to accumulate and leverage these assets, shielded by legal protections, becomes instrumental in achieving competitiveness and success. This transition toward intangibles-centric competitiveness has led to global dynamics where products and services grounded in IP and data exhibit negligible marginal production costs, fostering winner-take-most scenarios [16].

Moreover, the global business model has transformed from seller to buyer's market over the past two decades. This change implies an empowered and well-informed customer base actively shaping market dynamics. Consequently, business economics has shifted its focus inward, aligning with the resource-based view [17]. This perspective contends that a firm's distinctive resources and capabilities, including tangible and intangible assets, human capital, technology, and organizational processes, constitute the primary drivers of competitive advantage.

A seminal concept that gained prominence during this evolution is the idea of core competencies introduced by Hamel and Prahalad [19]. Core competencies denote unique capabilities and resources enabling a firm to establish and sustain a competitive advantage. Recognizing and nurturing these core competencies becomes paramount for long-term success as the bedrock for a firm's value proposition and differentiation in the marketplace [16]. This new perspective in business strategy represents a departure from external industry structures to a profound examination of organizations' internal resources and capabilities, particularly intangible assets. Thus, competitive advantage does not solely derive from different combinations of products and markets within an industry but is primarily attributed to variations in the possession of organizational resources [16]. Consistent with the resource-based view, competitive advantage arises from the strategic deployment of resources meeting specific criteria: value creation, rareness, inimitability, and nonsubstitutability. Intangible resources, identified as primary assets meeting these criteria, are termed in various ways, such as knowledge, invisible assets, core competencies, core capabilities, strategic assets, or intangible resources. Examples include elements like customer loyalty, technological expertise, or internal goodwill. These assets are often ignored or undervalued by accountants and strategists, but they hugely contribute to the competitiveness of companies, often more than tangible elements.

Recognizing the rise of intangible assets, organizations should understand that formulating a corporate strategy involves more than just analyzing competitive forces and industry dynamics, as proposed by Porter in the 1970s and 1980s. Moreover, the strategic importance of intangible assets extends beyond strategy development to execution processes [16].

The Widening Gap Between the Leaders and Laggards

In contrast to tangible assets like machinery or real estate, intangible assets, such as software or brand value, exhibit notable scalability and spillover effects. The scalability of these assets fosters investment due to their far-reaching impact and the potential for significant returns. However, the existence of spillover effects may deter average firms, raising concerns about competitors benefiting from their investments in intangibles. Despite potential drawbacks associated with spillovers, some solid and large companies excel at appropriating these effects through open innovation, leveraging the innovations of others to their advantage. This strategic capability can confer a competitive advantage, increasing productivity and profitability. The ability to absorb and effectively utilize spillovers may hinge on a firm's capacity to exploit synergies between various types of intangibles or adapt to the evolving settings of the intangible economy. This adaptation may require new institutional frameworks prioritizing lobbying, legal arguments, and institutional overhauls over immediate productivity that can be done only by large and competitive firms [14]. Consequently, the gap between the most and least productive firms continues to widen in the new era of intangible capitalism.

The rise of intangibles has created a scenario where being a mid-sized company is becoming less sustainable, as success in the intangible economy tends to create a virtuous circle where success breeds further success. The marginal cost of replicating intangibles is often minimal, exemplified by the low cost of producing an extra drug dose once it is developed [4]. This emphasizes the transformative nature of intangible assets and their impact on the competitive model and economic dynamics. The corporate strategy now resembles a competitive game where substantial rewards accrue primarily to the winners, and success is contingent on possessing a superior hand of intangibles [3, 5]. This trend has gained momentum over time, as data from different periods illustrate. The technology sector, dominated by a handful of giants like Google, Microsoft, Meta, and

Amazon, exemplifies how specific companies have achieved such dominance that competition from smaller and mid-sized companies is stifled [22].

Effective monopoly or duopoly is a defining feature of many sectors in the intangible economy, ranging from search engines and social media to personal computer and mobile device operating systems [1]. In the financial sector, a small number of large banks control a significant percentage of American banking assets. The period between 1997 and 2020 saw a decline of over 20 percent in the share of total revenue going to businesses with fewer than 100 employees [20]. Simultaneously, there has been a notable surge in the growth and consolidation of large multinational corporations across various sectors of the American economy. The *Wall Street Journal* reports that a third of industries are now considered highly concentrated [13]. This trend is not limited to the United States; European and Asian countries are experiencing similar consolidations.

In the last decade, the share of the world's economy controlled by large multinational corporations has surged. At the same time, competition from small- and medium-sized businesses has declined by a comparable factor. Consequently, a relatively small number of large corporations have increased their control over global markets, achieved higher profits, and effectively outcompeted their smaller rivals. Notably, tech giants have capitalized on their vast resources to gain market dominance and generate colossal revenues. A few companies, six or nine, manage the organization of the information economy from Internet search, advertising, and electronic retailing to clouding and social media. According to the McKinsey Global Institute, 10 percent of the world's public companies generate almost 80 percent of the profits [10]. For instance, those multinational corporations with more than U.S.$1 billion in annual revenue account for 60 percent of total global revenues [10].

Strategic Choices Unrelated to Price

In the current postindustrialized societies, basic consumer needs are mostly met, and there is a widespread abundance of goods. Therefore, businesses are facing increased global competition and cannot continue with the outdated traditional mass production methods. This transformation creates an ongoing challenge as companies strive to meet consumer demands for personalized and unique products. More and more, companies feel the need to enhance their efforts to secure monopoly profits or comparative advantages by any means [12]. Facing this situation, corporate strategies have shifted away from competing primarily on price. Instead, there is a greater focus on nonprice competitive factors such as reputation, branding, and tactics aimed at dominating the market to gain benefits similar to a monopoly. These strategies often involve increasing switching costs through proprietary platform technologies and innovative IPR management. The digital revolution has been crucial in combining large-scale production advantages with the global delivery of highly personalized products and services.

Contrary to expectations, globalization has not led to the standardization of products and services or the convergence of consumer preferences. Instead, it has expanded the choices available to consumers. This is evident in the diverse portfolios of global consumer giants like Coca-Cola and McDonald's and business services firms like IBM, which now have around 150 mostly local brands [12].

In the era of intangible capitalism, a new generation of business models places less emphasis on economies of scale and more on adaptability and agility in leveraging innovation, arbitrage opportunities, and scope effects. The primary focus has shifted toward creatively using intangible assets, quasi-assets, and competencies, particularly unique knowledge-based capabilities. The changing economic model has redirected business strategies toward monopolistic approaches, emphasizing nonprice competitive factors. Simultaneously, the digital revolution has enabled the global delivery of personalized products and services, providing consumers with various choices.

Converting Intangible Assets Into Competitive Advantage

Managing intangible assets becomes challenging due to contested ownership and the spillover of benefits, often leading to disputes over who owns them and the advantages they provide extending beyond their immediate holders. While many companies possess intangible assets, not all effectively convert them into intangible capital, which is essential for realizing their total value. In the intangible economy, transforming these assets into IP, networks, brands, and talent is crucial, as they constitute the precious resources that drive success [6].

The importance of IP should not be underestimated. Microsoft's global dominance, for instance, is mainly attributed to its IP in software programs, and pharmaceutical companies heavily rely on patents to protect their drugs. The growth of patenting has outpaced overall economic trends in the past two decades, highlighting the increasing organization of science and the growing recognition of the potential value embedded in IP.

The value of networks is unparalleled when they represent well-structured relationships with customers, suppliers, or other entities in the value chain. Customer relationships are often underestimated as a source of value. In sectors like integrated banking, companies understand that the true advantage lies in their products and existing relationships with a substantial customer base. Similarly, established telecommunications companies realize that, while their infrastructure holds value, their preexisting customer relationships are even more invaluable [7].

Brands are increasingly recognized as significant profit sources. Companies with strong brands, like Disney or Virgin, consistently generate higher returns compared to those without. In the food retail industry, where companies are deeply involved in every aspect of the value chain, the most lucrative segment is often found in brand management, leading some to exit other segments where capturing intangibles is more challenging.

Acknowledging the importance of talent, more companies are investing in well-organized systems to attract, retain, and develop top employees. Establishing a competitive advantage involves recruiting high-caliber talent, retaining them, and fostering their development. Companies implementing effective talent management practices generally outperform their industry peers regarding total return to shareholders [6, 7].

Cybersecurity and Espionage as Factors of Competitiveness

Intangible assets cover various valuable company elements, including software algorithms, brand identity, customer data, and organizational capital. These assets, often called *trade secrets*, are becoming a significant concern for companies due to the increasing risks associated with employee leaks, theft by competitors, and cyberattacks. The estimated annual cost of these risks is up to U.S.$1.7 trillion [11]. Companies facing cyber incidents often hesitate to disclose them, as they may face legal consequences and the threat of shareholder lawsuits. The fear of attracting further criminal activities also discourages organizations from revealing such incidents. A well-known example is Sony, which faced subsequent attacks after a breach in its PlayStation Network in 2011, highlighting the risks associated with publicizing cyber incidents [2].

The EIU Trade Secrets Survey (2022) identifies cybersecurity and employee leaks as the most significant threats globally to companies' trade secrets. Third-party leaks are particularly troubling in the United States, Singapore, and China, where respondents express dissatisfaction with the contractual protections for trade secrets. Different sectors have varying concerns, with cybersecurity being a top concern for energy, manufacturing, and technology sectors, while employee risks are prominent in consumer goods, retail, finance, and life sciences sectors. Managers consider cybersecurity weaknesses the top threat, and the connection between trade secret theft and corporate *bring your own device* policies is seen as potentially risky. Cases of trade secret misappropriation linked to employment litigation have risen recently, emphasizing the need to address insider threats [9].

A trade secret, representing valuable information known to a limited group, is essential for gaining a competitive advantage. However, challenges arise as many companies struggle to formally recognize proprietary information as trade secrets, limiting their legal capacity to protect these critical assets. The impact of the COVID-19 pandemic has heightened concerns, prompting organizations to prioritize trade secret protection as an *essential priority* [9].

Employees identified as critical sources of leaks present a complex challenge, especially in the era of remote work. The risk of accidental exposure or deliberate leaks is heightened by layoffs and redundancies, increasing the potential for intentional employee threats. Companies are actively prioritizing cybersecurity efforts, using strategies like digital watermarks and encryption. The regulation of employee activities, including surveillance, emerges as a crucial obstacle to preventing internal threats, particularly in the technology, media, and telecommunications sectors.

To strengthen protection against trade secret theft, companies are emphasizing strengthening policies and procedures, including tools like nondisclosure agreements and work-for-hire obligations. Proactive strategies, such as limiting access to confidential information, are recognized as effective measures, yet only half of executives tend to implement such practices. Companies are adopting a dual approach, restricting physical and digital access to vital documents and emphasizing confidentiality through regular reminders and comprehensive training initiatives.

Geographic Concentration and Importance of Clusters in Competitiveness

While some speculated that advancements in transportation and communication technologies might diminish the relevance of business clusters, historical evidence and economic theory present a contrasting narrative. Factors such as the mobility of IP and knowledge spillovers continue to foster geographical concentration. Intangible assets span various services and activities before and after manufacturing, including education, postproduction services, and initiatives to cultivate customer loyalty. These activities are the primary sources of value and competitive advantage for enterprises driven by intangible assets [8].

Geographically, intangible activities tend to cluster in core regions, with prominent companies centralizing their intellectual functions, contributing to the growth of headquarters in pivotal locations. Specialized firms, particularly finance, law, and marketing, often congregate in distinct districts. Certain cities wield significant dominance on the global economic stage due to their active engagement in business sectors such as financial and business services and corporate control and coordination functions [22].

Moreover, high-tech industries, grounded in a robust foundation of scientific knowledge, exhibit a proclivity toward clustering. However, it is crucial to note that not all high-tech firms can be equated with enterprises primarily based on intangible assets [8]. Knowledge spillovers, local labor pools, and collective learning experiences become more pronounced within tightly knit geographic clusters. The prominence of intangible assets within the organizational dynamics of firms implies that physical proximity fosters organizational learning and adaptation. Customer-related intangibles, such as brands and specific locations, become driving forces for clustering similar enterprises. The concept of territorialization can be used to describe the process of territorial agglomeration, where economic viability is rooted in assets—practices and relationships—that are scarce and not easily or quickly replicated elsewhere. Therefore, it is evident that geographical proximity and concentration are particularly critical for intangibles related to innovation, such as IP, R&D, human capital, and customer-related assets [8].

Furthermore, companies seek to mitigate risks in the intangible economy by locating close to one another. This perspective reinforces the traditional wisdom that agglomeration economies include benefits from the possibility of risk-sharing among clustered firms [15]. The clustering of intangible assets within geographic proximity becomes a strategic imperative for companies operating in the intangible economy, amplifying the importance of spatial dynamics in shaping economic activities and innovation.

Intellectual Monopoly

In the 21st-century intangible economy, there has been a significant change in the business world characterized by the dominance of intellectual monopolies among major corporations. These monopolies, which control significant portions of society's knowledge, are a critical factor in the market capitalization of top corporations. They continuously expand their control over knowledge, creating what is termed *knowledge rents*. Unlike traditional wealth accumulation, the concentration of capital in this era is primarily driven by aggregating intangible assets. In this context, intellectual monopolies do not necessarily monopolize markets in the conventional sense but achieve a monopolistic status by systematically and significantly controlling knowledge. This ongoing reinforcement of knowledge monopolies breaks the traditional link between innovation and growth.

Consequently, the concentration of intangible assets weakens the connection between innovation and growth while increasing corporate profit share [21]. Significant corporations, especially in the digital sector, concentrate profits and capital by capitalizing on knowledge and data monetization. The digital economy is characterized by a significant imbalance, with a small number of major players, such as GAFAM (Google and others), exerting substantial influence over market capitalization. The impact of the concentration of intangible assets is not limited to digital industries but extends to sectors like health care and pharmaceuticals. Industries such as ICT and health care play a crucial role in driving the intellectual monopolies, making their presence known across various sectors. In pursuit of intellectual rents, intellectual monopolies broaden their sources through predatory practices, shaping the dynamics of contemporary business competitiveness [21]. Intellectual monopolies transcend market influence; they function as capitalist planners orchestrating long-term capital accumulation beyond their legally owned capital. These entities control the production and innovation processes of subordinate firms, universities, and public research organizations. This control comprises crucial parameters, the setting of R&D agendas, and the regulation of various aspects within the innovation ecosystem. Thus, innovation transcends mere technical changes; political, social, and economic factors inherently influence it. Political decisions intertwine with economic interests, dictating innovation's direction, prioritization, and perceived boundaries.

Concluding Remarks

This chapter offered insights into the effects of intangible capitalism on strategic management and competitiveness. In the following chapter, we will focus on the implications of intangible economy for specific functions such as accounting, finance, and investment.

CHAPTER 8

Finance, Accounting, and Investment

Introduction

With their distinctive characteristics, intangible assets are anticipated to influence finance, accounting, and investment decisions significantly. Thus, this chapter examines the ramifications of intangible assets in various aspects, including accounting measures and firms' valuations, financial stability/instability, goodwill valuation, amortization, and the reliability of book and market values.

Inaccurate Accounting and Valuations

In the past, methods for assessing business performance were designed when companies mainly dealt with physical assets within well-defined boundaries. However, the modern economy has evolved, and businesses operate beyond traditional limits. This shift has resulted in a significant gap in measurement within national and corporate accounting systems [4]. Despite the perceived value of intangible assets, their limited recognition under Generally Accepted Accounting Principles (GAAP) poses challenges for verification. The incomplete measures currently used to assess intangibles create an information gap, potentially leading to suboptimal decision making and market inefficiencies.

A survey of senior accountants across various firms indicates widespread limitations in planning, recording, and analyzing intangible expenditures [8]. While many acknowledge the importance of intangibles for revenue generation, systematic measurement efforts are not joint, and ad hoc methods often guide managerial decisions. The lack of GAAP guidance makes firms responsible for identifying and classifying intangible expenditures. Therefore, there is a need for tools to measure intangible inputs and connect them to the final output for informed managerial decisions.

When companies acquire intangibles externally, such as patents or customer lists, these assets receive proper recognition. However, internally generated intangibles, like software or designs, are often categorized as expenses. This accounting inconsistency can potentially obscure a significant portion of intangible investments. The increasing prevalence of intangible investments has made financial accounts less informative. This issue leads to a declining correlation between book and market values, especially with rising R&D expenses [6]. It is crucial to enhance conventional metrics and systems to capture the value and impact of intangible assets and knowledge-based investments, requiring the development of new metrics to bridge this measurement gap and obtain a more accurate understanding of economic production [4].

Within the GAAP framework, expenses related to intangible assets are not adequately represented in financial statements [7, 8]. Evidence on the role of intangibles in generating output relies on imprecise metrics, including the gap between a company's market value of equity and book value of equity, R&D expenditures, and incomplete GAAP assessments of intangible assets. While some companies recognize the significance of intangibles and measure specific aspects for managerial decision making, there is a need for more widespread initiatives to establish a clear link between intangible expenditures and desired outcomes. The limited and fragmented analysis of intangible expenditures raises concerns about an information gap, potentially leading to distorted valuations, suboptimal decision making, and market inefficiencies [1, 8].

The uncertainty surrounding intangible investments has significant implications for their valuation and financing. The unclear valuation and inherent riskiness of intangible assets limit the efficiency of financing such ventures. Additionally, financing challenges linked to intangible assets are exacerbated by the substantial sunk costs usually required for their development. Companies with significant intangible assets may face difficulties securing financing, mainly through debt, as banks prefer tangible assets as collateral due to their seizure and sale potential in case of default.

The Speculative Nature of Intangibles and Financial Instability

In intangible markets, discrete transactions unfold, establishing a precise balance between buyers and sellers. Conversely, transactions form a continuous process in intangible markets, fostering sophisticated relationships between goods and prices. The nature of intangible assets, mainly information, leads to multiple sellers for a single buyer and vice versa, creating rapid information diffusion and a constant disequilibrium between buyers and sellers. Information markets operate in an environment of structural abundance, where every economic activity generates more information than it consumes. Thus, the interplay between information supply and demand results in a self-sustaining and ever-expanding growth spiral [12].

Another factor contributing to the instability of financial markets in an intangible economy is their anticipatory nature. Intangible capitalism operates on a speculative foundation, primarily based on future expectations. This framework's valuation processes and economic decisions heavily depend on anticipated future profits and projections [11]. An example of this speculative nature is seen in how companies are valued based on expected profits, primarily through metrics like price-to-earnings (P/E) ratios. Many mergers and acquisitions are driven not by current performance but by anticipating future profits, often represented by the intangible asset of goodwill. In the modern economy, a significant portion of the value attributed to companies in the S&P 500 comes from goodwill, accounting for approximately 84 percent of their total value in 2018 [11]. Goodwill impairment, referring to the diminished value of goodwill on a company's balance sheet, is crucial. In 2020, U.S. public companies recorded a total goodwill impairment of U.S.$142.5 billion, emphasizing its significant impact [9]. Management's discretionary judgment plays a crucial role in deciding whether goodwill impairment is necessary, affecting a company's income statement and balance sheet, reducing reported asset value, and potentially impacting reported earnings. A goodwill impairment charge may also negatively affect a company's financial ratios and be seen as a sign of financial distress.

The current financial systems are marked by procyclicality, where asset values are influenced by the influx of funds into the market. This characteristic contributes to capital asset inflation, where assets are over-valued due to expectations and speculation. Globalization and the digitalization of financial markets worsen the procyclical nature of intangible capitalism, affecting the relationship between asset values and household demand. Existing financial regulations are not well equipped to handle the procyclical dynamics inherent in intangible capitalism and its heavy reliance on future expectations. Adding to the challenge is the fact that financial regulations often focus on national economies, ignoring the global nature of markets. As a result, the speculative nature of modern intangible capitalism, combined with an inadequate response to maintaining the fictional consumer, has created an unstable and crisis-prone economic system [11].

Volatility in financial markets results in significant value fluctuations and creates a persistent gap between financial and economic value. Disparities between financial and economic value are observed in equity markets, contributing to the reluctance of many companies to list on public exchanges [5].

The Challenges of Measuring Intangible Assets in Business Combinations

Determining the value of intangible assets in business combinations is a complex task. The acquiring entity must record identifiable assets and liabilities at their fair values, and this becomes challenging when evaluating intangible assets, which often lack an active market. The fair value determination involves three main approaches: the market approach, the income approach, and the cost approach [13].

The market approach assesses an asset's fair value by comparing it to similar assets traded in recent market transactions. However, intangible assets often change hands in business sales or licensing agreements, limiting observable market data. Even when a quoted price exists, it may not accurately reflect fair value due to market illiquidity or other factors. Therefore, the market approach is less commonly used for intangible assets in business combinations [13].

The income approach estimates the present value of an asset's future economic benefits while incorporating as much observable market data as possible. This method heavily relies on projected financial information and utilizes discount rates [13].

The cost approach determines fair value by evaluating the monetary amount needed to repurchase or recreate the asset. Cost-based approaches are considered less robust than market or income approaches. Determining the cost of replacing or reproducing an intangible asset can be challenging, especially if the asset is unique. Cost-based measures may overlook the future economic benefits of owning the asset, potentially affecting a willing buyer's price.

Establishing fair value requires professional judgment based on assumptions and estimates tailored to the specific transaction. Different parties may reach different conclusions when assessing the same intangible asset. Fair value measurement introduces a *gray area* of uncertainty, representing a range of prices where hypothetical market transactions could occur. Every fair value estimate should contain specific fundamental conceptual characteristics despite this variability.

Measuring intangible assets in business combinations poses challenges due to their unique nature. The absence of an active market complicates determining fair value, leading to subjective judgments and estimates that may impact valuation accuracy. The complexity of intangible assets requires considering various valuation models, including the income, market, and cost approaches. Valuing intangible assets involves significant estimation, with uncertainties arising from future cash flows, discount rates, and assumptions about helpful life. Rapid technological advancements in technology-driven industries may quickly render existing intangible assets obsolete, making it challenging to predict future values. Compliance with legal and regulatory requirements adds complexity, especially considering that intangible assets often involve legal rights.

After a business combination, integrating and managing acquired intangible assets introduces new challenges. Aligning these assets with the acquirer's business operations demands meticulous planning and execution. Unlike tangible assets, intangibles may lack transaction history or pricing data, increasing reliance on assumptions. Intangible assets often include elements related to workforce expertise and intellectual capital, making the assessment and quantification of human capital subjective and challenging in attributing specific contributions to overall business value.

Identifiable and Unidentifiable Intangible Assets

Accounting standards are crucial in distinguishing between identifiable and unidentifiable intangible assets, whether acquired externally or developed internally by companies. Some intangible assets, like patents, franchises, and trademarks, are easily identifiable, while others lack apparent specificity. Identifiable assets can be acquired individually, as part of a group, or as components of an entire enterprise. On the other hand, unidentifiable assets, notably goodwill, cannot be independently acquired and represent the excess cost of an acquired enterprise over its identifiable net assets.

The classification of intangible assets into identifiable and unidentifiable categories depends on their exchangeability. Identifiable assets with legal or contractual status allowing sale, transfer, licensing, or rental include patents, copyrights, trademarks, trade secrets, and brands. Financial Accounting Standards (FAS) provide explicit criteria for identifying intangible assets, focusing on separability and legal-contractual status tests. Separability is met when an asset can be isolated and exchanged for value, such as a customer list acquired in a business combination.

Assets meeting the contractual legal criterion must be recognized separately from goodwill, even if they lack transferability or separability. This emphasizes the importance of legal or contractual status in distinguishing between identifiable and unidentifiable intangible assets.

Under the purchase method, intangible assets acquired in a business combination are recorded at a fair price. This differs from the pooling-of-interests method, which treats entities as if they continuously operated as one. Intangible assets can be obtained through acquisitions and internal development, like R&D initiatives. If assets are internally developed without a purchase, their valuation is determined as if a purchase occurred, based on fair value.

While accounting standards do not prescribe a specific method for computing fair value, they recommend using the best available evidence, often reflected in an active market price. While a preferred valuation method involves a net present value (NPV) calculation, the FASB allows alternative methods aligned with the three fundamental valuation approaches. This flexibility enables businesses to adopt diverse valuation techniques while following the accounting standards framework [3].

The Valuation of Goodwill

Goodwill, the most common form of unidentifiable intangible assets, arises as a transaction's residual element. It is explicitly defined as the "excess of the cost of an acquired enterprise over the sum of identifiable net assets." In simpler terms, goodwill represents the intangible value that cannot be precisely attributed to identifiable assets. It is important to note that goodwill is not the only type of unidentifiable intangible asset in accounting. This recognition comes from internally developed assets that currently defy specific identification. For instance, consider a company with a mentoring culture where senior executives impart valuable knowledge to younger employees, resulting in cost savings in design. The increased profitability may not be directly traceable to identifiable assets. In the case of an acquisition, this intangible asset, like the mentoring culture, would be implicitly included within goodwill. In other words, unidentifiable intangible assets within a firm become part of goodwill upon acquisition. These assets may initially escape identification and be treated as goodwill, or efforts may be made to pinpoint and separate them from goodwill [3].

From a different perspective, while goodwill is the primary classification for unidentifiable intangible assets from acquisitions, it does not negate the existence of other internally developed intangible assets that might also fall under goodwill until they can be distinctly identified and separated.

In the complex world of business transactions, goodwill takes center stage as a unique category of intangible asset, representing the unattributable value from the acquisition of an enterprise. It emerges as the residue when the cost of acquiring an enterprise exceeds the sum of its identifiable net assets. Goodwill encapsulates the intangible essence that escapes specific assignments to individually identifiable assets within the acquired entity.

Thus, unidentifiable intangible assets within a firm, whether arising from acquisitions or cultivated internally, converge under the overarching label of goodwill. The challenge lies in distinguishing these elusive assets, which may initially defy precise identification, highlighting the nuanced treatment of such assets in accounting and financial valuation. The ongoing challenge is to balance recognizing the intrinsic value of these intangibles with the need to quantify and allocate them within financial reporting standards accurately.

The Amortization and Impairment of Intangible Assets

Amortization and impairment are crucial aspects affecting the valuation of a company's intangible assets, which are disclosed on the balance sheet. Similar to tangible assets, intangibles have an estimated lifespan and experience a decrease in value over time. Amortization is the accounting method that systematically reflects this decrease over the asset's useful life. The company establishes a present value for the intangible asset and defines its anticipated useful life, like calculating depreciation for tangible assets. The annual amortization amount is then subtracted from the asset's value on the balance sheet. This adjustment is made through a debit entry to the amortization expense account and a corresponding credit to the contra account, known as accumulated amortization, reported on the balance sheet. The amortization expense is also recognized on the income statement as an operating cost, impacting net income, a key metric used in calculating earnings per share.

Amortization has a significant effect on evaluating a company's financial performance. As it directly influences reported net income, any misjudgment in estimating the asset's salvage value and useful life can substantially impact the company's bottom line. Recognizing its pivotal role, new accounting principles mandate annual reassessment of intangible asset values. If, during this reassessment, the fair value is determined to be less than the intangible asset's current valuation minus the amortization expense, the asset is deemed impaired. In the event of impairment, the difference between fair value and the current value is recorded as an impairment charge, adjusting the intangible asset's value on the balance sheet to reflect its accurate, fair market value. This method ensures transparency and accuracy in financial reporting, providing investors with crucial insights into the genuine value of a company's intangible assets.

For assets with indefinite useful lives, like goodwill and certain brands or trade secrets, an annual impairment test is conducted to ensure their fair value is accurately reflected in financial statements. Specific events or changes in circumstances trigger these tests, such as a significant decrease in market price, adverse changes in use or physical condition, legal factors, business climate, unexpected costs, current-period operating losses, or an expectation of selling the asset before its estimated useful life. To illustrate, when a brand is discontinued, the associated trademark value may become impaired.

When a company acquires another's assets, the acquired goodwill may decrease in value, leading to an impairment cost recorded on the acquiring company's books. Responsible handling of impairment costs ensures accurate valuations for investors, as the complexity of determining amortization and life expectancy of intangible assets can potentially be manipulated. A contributing factor to this manipulation is that declared values of intangible assets are not required to be reported.

The Increasing Divergence Between Book Value and Market Value

In the dynamic world of the intangible economy, creating and managing intangible assets have become central, challenging the traditional belief that economic value comes solely from tangible goods production. This shift is reflected in financial statements, which are now seen as less informative about a company's current financial status and future potential. The growing gap between market value and book value of equity emphasizes this changing economic setting, with a significant portion of market value not captured in traditional balance sheets. Scholars like Lev and Zarowin [10] argue that this indicates a revolutionary change in economic value creation and a decline in the relevance of traditional financial metrics [2, 10].

Many thriving startups and unicorns like Uber, Airbnb, and SpaceX gain valuation and go public not solely based on their tangible outputs but primarily on the strength of their intangible assets. These startups incorporate distinctive ideas, IPs, inventive solutions, and exclusive technologies. The capacity to generate and safeguard IP empowers these firms to forge competitive edges, ultimately drawing in investment. As intangibles become increasingly crucial in determining a company's success, there is a rising call for changes or expansions to the traditional accounting model. This includes a demand for adapting accounting standards to include intangibles, alliances, partnerships, financial instruments, and other emerging challenges. Rethinking how various intangibles are measured and treated becomes crucial to enhancing the overall usefulness of accounting information in this evolving economic model. The frequent occurrence of mergers and acquisitions, both domestically and internationally, emphasizes the importance of goodwill and the complexities in its accounting practices [14]. Many international mergers and acquisitions are driven by pursuing a competitive advantage rooted in technology, knowledge, and other intangible assets. However, different countries' varied criteria for recognizing, measuring, and depreciating intangible assets can impact certain firms' ability to attract capital in financial markets. For example, the full expensing of goodwill could disadvantage firms from specific countries in business acquisition scenarios against foreign competitors, affecting reported earnings.

Recognizing the vital role of intellectual capital as a key value driver, managers are urged to identify the fundamental drivers of their firms' value and enhance their influence on future performance. Standard-setting bodies are grappling with developing guidelines to facilitate decision-making processes for business enterprise managers and capital providers. These guidelines aim to identify intangible elements, establish valuation criteria, create new financial reporting standards, and provide guidance for measuring and effectively managing intangibles within firms. Addressing these challenges is crucial for navigating the global business environment and ensuring fair competition and transparency in financial markets [2].

Empirical evidence from multiple studies indicates a noticeable decline in the utility of financial reports over the years. This reduced effectiveness is particularly evident in the decreasing explanatory power of earnings, contrasted with the growing significance of book values. The changing setting, both internal and external to corporations, along with heightened uncertainty, substantially contributes to the diminishing informativeness of financial reports.

One significant risk arises when companies underinvest in intangibles, which are crucial for maintaining or gaining market share and reinforcing competitive positions. A positive correlation between R&D investments and market value emphasizes the critical importance of effectively identifying and managing intangibles. Although widely used, traditional indicators such as R&D and patents present limitations, failing to capture the dynamic nature of R&D activities and provide a comprehensive view of a firm's innovative capabilities. Varied research results on the relationship between R&D and corporate performance indicate the necessity for a nuanced approach to understanding and leveraging these investments. Furthermore, the valuation of brand names has gained prominence, sparking debates around various methods, including historical cost, market value, premium price, NPV, and brand strength. Additionally, covenants not to compete are recognized as assets carrying potential tax benefits.

Despite their critical role, financial reporting often neglects human assets, leading to periodic debates on their accounting treatment. Recent research highlights the significance of recognizing intellectual capital, particularly in knowledge-based service firms. Empirical evidence supports a positive association between human resource investments and future performance, highlighting the need for their acknowledgment in financial reporting. The immediate expensing of intangible investments introduces risks of undervaluing companies. Studies reveal mispricing due to inadequate reporting on intangibles, impacting investment decisions, mergers, acquisitions, and lending practices. The evolving business model necessitates a shift in accounting models to provide stakeholders with accurate, relevant, and comparable financial information. This shift ensures informed decision making and efficient resource allocation in contemporary corporate finance's dynamic and complex field [2].

Concluding Remarks

In conclusion, we have proposed in this chapter that the advent of intangible capitalism instigates a paradigm shift in finance and accounting.

Consequently, conventional accounting and financial metrics may lose accuracy or even relevance. In the subsequent chapter, our focus will shift to another vital business domain: marketing, consumption, and innovation, where we will continue to explore the far-reaching impacts of the intangible economy.

CHAPTER 9

Consumption, Marketing, and Innovation

Introduction

Consumption, marketing, and innovation are pivotal business functions significantly impacted by the ascendance of intangible assets. In this chapter, we propose that the intangible economy has ushered in a new paradigm of consumption, where consumers play a central role in the production process. Additionally, we explore the phenomena of market intangiblization, hyperreality, and delusion within this novel economic landscape, explaining how intangible assets reshape innovation and design. The abundance of intangible products in the intangible economy emphasizes the crucial marketing task of capturing consumer attention.

Capitalizing on Data

In the intangible economy, businesses strategically use data assets to boost product sales by offering personalized recommendations and targeted advertising. Amazon, for example, utilizes user data for collaborative filtering, resulting in significant profit margin increases. Similarly, Walmart leverages self-collected data, reporting substantial income growth online after establishing Walmart's Data Lab. Social media giants like Facebook and Tencent use diverse user datasets for targeted advertising [18]. The role of data assets goes beyond marketing, influencing product pricing, logistics management, and overall service design. Amazon and Walmart use consumer data for efficient inventory management, adapting swiftly to market trends. Walmart integrates blockchain technology for food safety, recording transaction details to monitor the entire production and retail cycle. Social media platforms continuously evolve through data analysis, contributing to ongoing service improvements. For instance, Facebook encourages users to share music preferences, refining targeted advertising, while Tencent's instant messaging apps and WeChat facilitate rapid design and service improvements. Companies also offer additional services based on their self-collected data assets. Amazon collaborates with third-party websites to enhance advertising efficiency, and Walmart uses Tencent's geographical location services to send targeted messages to consumers at stores.

In China, innovative applications of data assets are seen in the synergies between online payment platforms and social media. Alipay covers diverse transactions in consumers' daily lives, aiding credit providers in assessing borrowers' payment abilities. Tencent's gaming service generates revenue and gathers valuable user data, contributing significantly to revenue growth. Comparing U.S. and Chinese companies reveals distinct approaches to data asset utilization. U.S. companies focus on refining marketing capabilities and selling data, while Chinese counterparts like Alipay and WeChat Pay actively enhance financial services through efficient data analytics. U.S. technology firms are less involved in providing financial services, possibly influenced by the benefits and interest protection enjoyed by credit providers. By contrast, China's financial services offer room for improvement, presenting opportunities for private technology firms to play a more significant role.

Extracting business value from data assets requires targeted strategies across advertising, product and service design, client management, and innovative applications. The comparative analysis highlights the nuanced approaches adopted by U.S. and Chinese companies, emphasizing the proactive role of Chinese firms in advancing financial services through sophisticated data analytics.

The Intangible Consumption

In the last two decades, how people buy and use goods and services has dramatically changed. This shift is marked by the increasing blend of physical and virtual aspects, making products and services less tangible. Customers now have numerous options online and offline, giving them the power to research and acquire new products and services thoroughly.

Digital devices, once seen as extras, are now essential tools for businesses to promote, sell, and expand their market share [17].

Both business and consumer interactions and business interactions are experiencing a change in what customers expect. The focus now is on the quality of products or services based on speed, convenience, and ease of use [14]. As the pressure to adapt to the digitization of consumption increases, businesses strategically concentrate on three key areas to attract and keep customers: customer experience, personalization, and access ownership. Businesses understand that offering tangible products and services cannot captivate modern consumers. Instead, they use digital interfaces to create unique and impressive customer experiences, emphasizing the importance of memorable interactions to stand out from competitors.

Moreover, the digital era allows companies to provide personalized and highly customized products and services that align with individual preferences and needs. This level of personalization enhances customer engagement and fosters stronger brand loyalty.

The concept of ownership is also changing, with intangible ideas such as access and utility taking precedence [12]. Businesses are increasingly adopting models based on sharing, access, and convenience to cater to the changing preferences of their customer base. This shift in mindset aligns with evolving consumer behaviors and promotes a more sustainable and flexible approach to consumption. Data plays a crucial role in this digital setting, as businesses collect and use customer data to create digitally enabled revenue models. By tailoring products and services to align with consumers' specific needs, desires, and preferences, businesses can optimize their offerings and enhance customer satisfaction.

As a result, businesses find themselves compelled to engage customers through new digital channels to realize short-term profits and cultivate enduring and enjoyable digital experiences. Particularly for those operating in traditional industries, a significant investment in digitizing business processes becomes imperative to meet the heightened expectations of their digitally empowered customer base. This strategic adaptation ensures that businesses remain competitive and relevant in a rapidly evolving consumer environment driven by the convergence of physical and virtual spaces.

Prosumers: Consumers as Producers

The term *prosumer* in the digital economy comprehends individuals who engage in a dual role as consumers and producers of goods, services, or content. This amalgamation of *producer* and *consumer* indicates a departure from the traditional passive consumer model to one where individuals contribute actively to the creation, distribution, or enhancement of products and services [10]. This concept has gained prominence alongside the increasing prevalence of digital technologies and online platforms. This phenomenon arises from the interactive and participatory nature of digital technologies and the Internet. On the one side, consumers retain traditional behaviors such as evaluating, choosing, and paying for intangible products or services that align with their needs or preferences. Conversely, in the digital economy, consumers also embrace the role of producers, actively generating content, contributing to online platforms, and engaging in user-generated activities [11].

User-generated content, comprising reviews, comments, blog posts, and social media updates, has evolved into a pivotal digital economy component. Additionally, consumers contribute significantly to creating and distributing digital goods and services through various platforms. For instance, individuals can create and share videos on platforms like YouTube, provide reviews on e-commerce sites like Amazon, or even develop apps for mobile devices.

A notable aspect of this dual role is evident in consumers' involvement in developing and funding projects, products, or ideas, often utilizing crowdfunding platforms. This issue enables consumers to directly impact the production and introduction of offerings into the market. Social media becomes another avenue where consumers actively participate by creating and sharing content, connecting with others, and influencing trends. Many social media platforms thrive on user-generated content, emphasizing the symbiotic relationship between consumers and the digital ecosystem.

Moreover, consumers may actively engage in collaborative consumption models, leveraging platforms directly connecting producers and consumers. This participation extends beyond traditional economic transactions to include sharing resources and services. Thus, the concept of prosumers in the digital economy reflects a dynamic shift from passive consumption to active participation and contribution, shaping the evolving model of digital interactions and transactions.

Intangiblization of Markets

The way goods are consumed, produced, and traded between businesses is undergoing significant changes, leading to a fundamental market shift. While traditional markets focused on exchanging physical goods are still thriving, there is a notable transformation as markets increasingly involve trading intangible assets. This shift does not diminish the importance of markets for physical goods; instead, it amplifies the growth of intangible markets, influencing the development of markets for tangible goods [7].

In traditional markets for physical goods, transactions are discrete, involving distinct buyers and sellers. By contrast, intangible markets operate continuously, blurring the lines between buyers and sellers. Participants in intangible markets often assume dual roles as producers and consumers, such as academics exchanging data online or financial institutions operating within a trading network. Pricing intangibles poses a challenge, leading to unconventional practices like giveaways, subsidies, cross-subsidies, indirect payments, or bundled pricing structures. While some argue for a departure from traditional market models due to the unique characteristics of intangibles, we may suggest that the market for ideas should be approached similarly to the tangible goods market [4]. Another emerging viewpoint is to consider markets for tangible goods as a specialized case within the broader framework of markets for intangibles.

The once-clear distinction between markets for goods and intangibles is gradually fading, with all markets adopting more intangible characteristics. Financial markets exemplify this trend, experiencing significant growth over the past three decades. The daily volume of foreign exchange transactions, exceeding U.S.\$1,500 trillion, surpasses the daily volume of international trade in goods by over 70 times. The growth of international transactions, particularly in foreign exchange, has outpaced international trade in tangible goods.

Capital markets, involving equities and bonds, have become primary sources for funding technological innovation. This shift has accelerated the diffusion of innovation, reshaping traditional ideas of economic hierarchy and capital mobilization. The rapid expansion of these markets is closely tied to the widespread adoption of information technology, where intangible data, rather than physical products, constitutes the primary exchange. Advances in financial economics have led to derivative markets trading dematerialized versions of conventional products, expanding the concepts of tradeability and risk management. Derivative markets, including futures, options, and swaps, have grown faster than cash markets dealing in the underlying instruments [7, 15].

Consumption, Production, and Pricing

The intangible economy, marked by elements not confined to traditional physical forms, is experiencing a significant shift driven by technological progress. Technological advancements have greatly facilitated the creation and dissemination of intangible products, like digital content and information. These intangible entities, lacking a physical presence, can be easily duplicated and shared on a large scale. Technology is crucial in separating content from its physical form, allowing the same information to exist in diverse formats and be accessed through various platforms.

Intangible products, especially information, have distinct characteristics. They can be used simultaneously by multiple individuals without depletion; their consumption does not diminish the product, and one person's usage does not prevent others from enjoying the same product. These characteristics classify intangible artifacts as shared goods, transcending geographical boundaries and enabling diverse groups to partake in the same offerings. Sharing within the intangible economy does not imply uniformity. Different groups with varied preferences can simultaneously use the same intangible products, fostering diversity within the user base. This widespread sharing generates externalities, influencing individual choices and willingness to pay for intangible products based on the actions of others.

Like digital content creators, owners of intangible artifacts face challenges in controlling access and excluding nonpaying users. The intrinsic nature of these products complicates the enforcement of the traditional concept of exclusive ownership and consumption.

Sharing extends beyond the mere utilization of intangible products; it plays a pivotal role in their creation. Many intangible products result from collaborative efforts between consumers and producers. Consumers actively contribute to the content, and the ease of copying and separating content from support allows for unique combinations of contributions. This pervasive sharing challenges conventional perceptions of property ownership, giving rise to the concept of IP. The value of IP lies in facilitating widespread access and usage, extending beyond technology and science to involve artistic creations, brand management, and other intangible assets.

Pricing intangible artifacts poses challenges due to their unique economic characteristics. Production costs do not aptly guide pricing, as there is no direct correlation between inputs and outputs. Consumption levels more influence the scale of production than production quantities. Additionally, willingness to pay is affected by factors such as ease of copying and sharing, alongside other external considerations. Traditionally, pricing for intangibles was based on the support they received rather than their content. However, technological advancements now allow for separate pricing strategies, leading to a diverse range of pricing approaches based on the estimated value of the content. This includes selling, sharing, and giving away these intangible products. The shift toward content-based pricing makes the value of intangible artifacts more volatile compared to physical goods with more stable prices. Intangible products can experience substantial price fluctuations, and their value is highly time-sensitive. Effectively managing this volatility presents a challenge, requiring a delicate balance between efficiency and cost-effectiveness.

Hyperreality and the Power of Delusion

In the evolving intangible economy, the convergence of the virtual and physical worlds has ushered in an era known as hyperreality, a term coined by the French philosopher Jean Baudrillard [2]. Hyperreality blurs the boundary between reality and simulation, making it challenging to distinguish between the two. Thus, representations or simulations often carry more weight than actual reality.

In the business, symbols and simulated realities play a crucial role. Companies use them to build brand identities and marketing campaigns beyond the tangible aspects of their products or services. By creating immersive experiences, businesses develop simulated environments that feel more authentic than the physical world, shaping how consumers perceive their offerings.

In the digital age, e-commerce platforms establish virtual stores replicating traditional shopping experiences. Online shopping, with product visualization and interactive features, fosters a sense of hyperreality, blurring the lines between digital and physical retail spaces. Brands leverage virtual events, content, and entertainment experiences to connect with consumers in digital spaces, making these simulated experiences integral to brand identity and consumer engagement. In business and industry, virtual training programs use simulations to create hyperrealistic scenarios for employees to practice skills and decision making in situations mirroring the real world. Social media platforms contribute to hyperreality by shaping digital personas that may not fully represent individuals or businesses. Retail businesses harness augmented reality for virtual try-on experiences, allowing customers to visualize products before purchase and further eroding the boundary between physical and virtual shopping. In art, nonfungible tokens (NFTs) contribute to hyperreality, as digital art and collectibles in a virtual space possess real-world value.

However, as businesses increasingly engage consumers through simulations and digital experiences, concerns arise about the authenticity of these interactions and the potential disconnection from actual reality. Striking a balance between creating compelling virtual experiences and maintaining authenticity becomes a key challenge in navigating the hyperreality of the modern era.

More recently, businesses have embraced virtual and augmented reality technologies to create immersive experiences, enhance training, and engage customers innovatively. The Metaverse is emerging as a space for economic activities, including virtual commerce, digital real estate, and virtual events, offering new avenues for businesses to connect with consumers in a virtual environment. Cryptocurrencies have become integral to the intangible economy, providing decentralized and secure means of financial transactions. Blockchain technology, which underlies many cryptocurrencies, finds applications beyond finance, such as supply chain management and smart contracts.

Trust assumes paramount importance in this virtual, intangible, and sometimes delusional economy. The proliferation of fake news and deep fake content challenges maintaining trust and credibility in online interactions. Businesses and individuals must navigate the information environment carefully to safeguard their reputations. User experience holds significant sway, and visual or auditory illusions are employed in design and marketing to enhance the overall user experience of digital products and services.

The Shortening Product Life Cycles

The typical life cycle of a product follows four key stages: introduction, growth, maturity, and decline. In the decline stage, new and competitive products replace their predecessors. The rise of the intangible economy has accelerated innovation, leading to shorter product life cycle. This shift, characterized by a faster pace in the design, production, purchase, and consumption processes, disrupts stability by quickly making items, especially electronic devices, obsolete shortly after their introduction. In the past decade, the average lifespan of a computer has decreased from four or five years to just two years, resulting in a significant portion of sales for knowledge-intensive devices occurring soon after their introduction. This compression in product life cycles requires companies to maintain lean inventory levels and strategically reduce investments across their entire value chain [9].

Swift engineering changes are expected in all production stages, including supply chains and technological development. As product life cycles shorten, the introduction and growth stages merge, quickly followed by a steep decline. Essentially, the diminishing product life cycles indicate the disappearance of the maturity stage. The time to profit from a new product is brief, as competitors catch up swiftly, leading to diminishing profit margins. The rapid decline in product life cycles and the quick shift of users to next-generation products often leave businesses with limited time and resources to execute effective marketing campaigns [6].

To address the challenges posed by shortened product life cycles, manufacturers and upstream suppliers are increasingly embracing integration to enhance efficiencies [13]. Supply chain integration takes various forms, generally involving a collaborative process where two or more enterprises jointly execute activities within the supply chain [5].

In marketing, businesses must adopt strategic approaches to cope with accelerated product life cycles. Three key strategies emerge extensive marketing efforts, simultaneous targeting of various segments, and intensive marketing endeavors. The brevity of product life cycles necessitates swift data collection and processing for diverse market segments, enabling businesses to target them simultaneously. Moreover, firms must engage in more intensive, high-quality marketing campaigns to swiftly captivate customers in the fleeting window of opportunity [8].

The Interconnected Innovation

In the world of intangible capitalism, the creation of value primarily comes from the manipulation and transformation of ideas. This shift in value creation has revolutionized the model of innovation. Innovation is no longer limited to an individual working alone in a workshop but thrives within collaborative teams, often clustered in specific innovation hubs. These teams engage in a dynamic exchange of ideas with partners, suppliers, and customers, both locally and globally. The ease with which ideas and talented individuals move across international boundaries has turned innovation into a global activity.

This globalized approach to innovation has not only sped up technological development but has also uncovered numerous opportunities. Once confined to traditional innovation hubs in developed nations, creative individuals are now valued globally. There is greater recognition of new talent sources beyond established innovation hotspots, leading to a worldwide exchange of ideas and a global market for innovation talent. In conjunction with expanding international trade and FDI, talent mobility has become a defining feature of contemporary globalization. Renowned innovators are considered a critical resource, comparable in importance to precious resources like oil or water. This acknowledgment stems from the widely accepted notion that innovation in products and services is a significant, if not the predominant, driver of economic growth.

It is essential to understand that *innovation* goes beyond researchers' mere development of cutting-edge technologies in this setting. It includes the creative processes through which individuals refine, repackage, and combine technologies before bringing them to market. Amar Bhidé, a business professor at Columbia University, argues in his book, *The Venturesome Economy*, that the orchestration of innovation, involving the refinement and application of ideas, can be more influential in driving economic activity than pure research [3]. Bhidé contends that in a world where breakthrough ideas effortlessly transcend national borders, the origin of ideas becomes inconsequential [3]. Ideas cross borders not only in the form of research papers, e-mails, and web pages but also within the minds of talented individuals. Financial incentives do not solely drive this movement of talent; they may also be motivated by a desire for greater academic freedom, improved access to research facilities and funding, or the opportunity to collaborate with key researchers in a specific field.

Countries capable of attracting talented individuals benefit from accelerated economic growth, closer collaboration with the countries of origin, and the likelihood that immigrant entrepreneurs will establish new companies, creating jobs. Talent mobility establishes vital links between companies and sources of foreign innovation and research expertise, proving mutually beneficial. Immigrant workers bring valuable knowledge of their home markets, facilitating the entry of companies in the destination country into those markets.

However, the complex tapestry of talent mobility is woven with several concerns. In developed nations traditionally dependent on foreign talent, such as the United States, there is growing anxiety about the increasing difficulty of attracting talent as new opportunities emerge elsewhere. In developed nations like Germany, which historically have not relied heavily on foreign talent, the aging population and a decline in birth rates necessitate widening the talent supply as skilled workers exit the workforce and young people show less interest in technical subjects than before. In developing countries, where there is a substantial supply of new talent, the concern revolves around the graduates having a broad technical foundation but potentially lacking the specialized skills demanded by specific industries [1].

Abundance and the Increasing Value of Users' Attention

In the previous chapters, we examined the unique characteristics of intangible assets, covering aspects like minimal or no additional costs, extensive scalability, network effects, and partial exclusivity. These traits result in a surplus of intangible products, spanning digital media, software, online educational materials, e-books, apps, music, electronic artwork, and general information. Notably, software can be continuously sold without compromising its quality or availability. Likewise, a book has the potential to be sold to the entire global population, TV channels and entertainment content are produced more than actual demand, and consumers often lack the time and attention needed to engage with the intangible products they acquire or purchase entirely. This surplus defines intangible capitalism as an economy where production surpasses consumption, and user participation holds excellent value. Online platforms play a crucial role in fostering this surplus by providing vast data, educational content, and expertise. Additionally, sharing IP through licensing and collaboration enhances innovation, reinforcing the perception of abundance. The expanding user base on social media platforms amplifies their value, creating abundant connections, information exchange, and communication.

However, despite the infinite supply of intangibles, demand remains finite. While intangible production faces no limits, the number of users, whether a nation's or the global population, is inherently limited. In the context of this abundance and oversupply, users' attention emerges as a rare commodity, prompting businesses to compete fiercely. Attention, defined as allocating mental resources to visible or conceptual objects, is significant in marketing management. This concept can be divided into two major dimensions: intensity and duration. Over the past three decades, both the intensity and duration of consumers' attention have declined [16].

Our lives have become inundated with a multitude of audiovisual information from new media sources, including the Internet, mobile devices, radio, television, and newspapers. This saturation has led to increased distraction and a decline in attention. Platforms like Twitter, Facebook, and Snapchat have found success by offering short-format content to capture consumers' attention quickly. For instance, widespread among the young mobile generation, Snapchat positions itself with short and disposable content, hosting videos that are 10 seconds or shorter videos.

In addition to shorter attention spans, the quality of consumers' attention has deteriorated in recent decades, with indexes indicating a waning interest in the content of advertisements. Consumers can now obtain information on products, prices, and technical features from various sources, including company websites and peer evaluations, making webpages potential replacements for traditional advertisements. The price of high-quality attention has reportedly increased ninefold in the last two decades, a trend expected to continue in the increasingly crowded and competitive market for consumer attention. Given these dynamics, customers' attention is viewed as a precious commodity that requires careful management. In the face of intense competition, marketing managers must adapt their advertising strategies to the level of attention to enhance campaign success.

Concluding Remarks

This chapter highlighted several notable aspects of marketing, consumption, and innovation within the framework of the intangible economy. As we move to the next chapter, our attention shifts toward exploring the broader societal ramifications stemming from the rise of intangible capitalism. Through this exploration, we aim to dig deeper into understanding how intangible assets shape economic dynamics and influence social structures, values, and behaviors on a broader scale.

CHAPTER 10

Societal Implications

Living (and Outliving) in Intangible Capitalism

Introduction

Corporations have become the agents of societal change, and a close relationship exists between business and society. Recognizing this intricate relationship between business and society, our focus in this final chapter is dedicated to exploring the societal repercussions of intangible capitalism. Specifically, we delve into the impacts of intangible capitalism on critical issues such as inequality, the financialization of society and politics, the evolving nature of economic value, and psychological implications such as attention loss, addiction, and the distortion of perception and meaning. This examination aims to shed light on the intricate interplay between the economy and broader societal constructs.

The Rising Inequality: The Logic of All-or-Nothing

The increasing prevalence of intangible assets in the economy fosters various forms of inequality, including income, wealth, and social status. Inventors or entrepreneurs can capture much of the generated value when creating new intangible assets. However, the remaining value often goes to external investors or other entities. Concentrating the entrepreneur's share, which is not readily tradable, can result in inequality due to systematic risk and unforeseen shocks. Entrepreneurs must wait to sell future claims to intangibles in advance, leading to concentrated ownership. Conversely, external parties can claim ownership when the intangible is codified and stored, resulting in a more dispersed ownership structure.

The concentration of ownership in early-stage intangibles contributes to increasing inequality.

Additionally, investments in intangible assets, such as management practices, may be tied to key employees. As the significance of intangibles grows in firms' capital stocks, the cash flows generated by these assets are shared between shareholders and critical talent, potentially causing inequality between key workers and other employees, especially when the value is specific to the firm. The portion of returns to key talent is not constant and depends on their external opportunities, introducing another source of inequality. Furthermore, intangibles can contribute to income inequality by accentuating the complementarity between capital and skills. If intangibles boost the productivity of high-skilled labor, their growing importance may increase income inequality. Empirical evidence indicates that pay for high-skilled labor, especially equity pay, has increased in industries highly exposed to declining investment goods prices, suggesting a correlation between intangibles and income inequality.

The ascent of intangibles also contributes to wealth inequality by driving up property prices in thriving cities. Some cities have become hubs for intangible-driven economic activities due to spillovers and synergies, making them attractive to businesses and individuals. Intangibles are more mobile than tangible assets, making it challenging for governments to tax them effectively. Capital gains, often derived from intangibles, may be taxed lower than income in certain countries. This competition in taxation between jurisdictions diminishes governments' capacity to implement redistributive policies, exacerbating wealth inequality. The economic changes brought about by intangibles also contribute to social and attitudinal inequality, as individuals with varying psychological traits, such as openness to experience, may behave differently in an intangible-driven economy. This division in psychological traits correlates with political divides and contributes to a sense of alienation and estrangement between different social groups.

Financialization

In contemporary times, finance has shifted from being a supportive service for the economy to becoming a substantial sector in its own right.

Traditionally, the financial sector's primary role was to aid economic activities by providing essential services like capital allocation, risk management, and payment systems. However, in the era of the intangible economy, finance has evolved into a sector with its dynamics, influencing the broader economy significantly. Financialization, the increased dominance of financial markets, institutions, and motives, highlights the expanding influence of finance beyond merely supporting economic activities.

Over time, finance has not only served as a support mechanism but has become a driver of profit-seeking activities independently. The rise of complex financial instruments like derivatives and securitization has allowed financial institutions to engage in complex and often speculative transactions. Securitization involves transforming original securities into more sophisticated forms. At the same time, derivatives derive their value from the market value of other securities, showcasing their complexity, opacity, and disconnection from the tangible economy. Originally designed to manage risks, these financial instruments have evolved into tools for generating profits independently of real economic activities. The focus has shifted from traditional lending and investment to trading and manipulating financial products.

Various financial intermediaries, such as investment banks, hedge funds, and private equity firms, have emerged, contributing to the financial sector's growing autonomy from its traditional role as an economic facilitator. Operating on a global scale due to the globalization of financial markets, these institutions have become multinational conglomerates, operating across borders and not confined to serving the interests of a single national economy.

The combination of the intangible economy and financialization has led to an increase in short-termism. The financial sector's focus on short-term gains, driven by quarterly profit expectations and performance metrics, has shifted attention toward quick returns rather than long-term investment in productive activities. Technological innovations like algorithmic trading and high-frequency trading have further transformed financial transactions, allowing finance to operate with unprecedented speed and complexity, sometimes detached from the real-world economic activities they were meant to support.

The cumulative effect of these changes has turned finance into a sector that serves and significantly influences the broader economy. This transformation raises concerns about the potential consequences of financial activities prioritizing short-term gains and speculative activities over the long-term health and stability of the overall economy.

The Financial Markets Paradox

The financial markets paradox is a significant aspect of the intangible economy, representing a crucial contradiction [5]. Financial markets, hailed as a success in the market paradigm, embody the ideals of abundant information and cost-effectiveness in a perfect market. They function globally, operate 24/7, involve a diverse range of participants, and offer detailed economic information at decreasing transaction costs. However, despite these positive aspects, there is widespread dissatisfaction with the seemingly unstoppable rise of financial markets. This discontent extends beyond left-leaning politicians and includes economic policymakers, market regulators, and industry practitioners. The dissatisfaction revolves around three major accusations. First, financial markets are seen as too powerful, influencing economic policy and often prioritizing short-term gains over long-term development, creating a perceived *dictatorship of financial markets*. Second, markets are considered excessively volatile, displaying widespread, persistent, and contagious fluctuations in financial prices across various segments such as foreign exchange, interest rates, and equities. Third, financial markets are accused of sending inaccurate signals about economic performance and value, contributing to a focus on short-term financial metrics rather than sustainable, long-term objectives [5].

Dematerialization

The impact of the intangible economy is extensive, touching various sectors and activities. While it does not eliminate traditional areas like agriculture or industry, it significantly transforms how firms, markets, and transactions are structured. This transformation challenges established economic principles, particularly by introducing disequilibrium instead of the traditional emphasis on equilibrium [5]. Dematerialization is marked by three main characteristics: abundance, interpenetration, and indeterminacy.

First, the intangible economy is structurally abundant. Unlike the industrial economy, where physical goods decay and consumption marks the end of their economic life, intangible artifacts are inexpensive to replicate and endure beyond consumption. This abundance extends the reach of popular intangible artifacts compared to material goods. Second, the boundaries between sectors like telecommunications, informatics, electronics, and audio-visual entertainment overlap, blurring traditional distinctions. This interpenetration challenges the separation between work and leisure, home and workplace, and other previously distinct categories. Third, the intangible economy operates on fuzzy logic, with overlapping instead of binary exclusivity. This leads to porous, overlaying, and unstable boundaries between various aspects of the economy.

The overflow of information, images, messages, and transactions due to a mismatch between the supply and demand of intangible items results in what is known as an *info glut*. This situation is worsened by deregulation and technological advancements, causing overwhelming data. Dealing with this abundance leads to new ways of consumption like zapping, surfing, or browsing, characterized by a short attention span and unpredictability, challenging traditional distinctions. The surplus of information also contributes to shorter product cycles, making obsolescence a key factor. In fields like microcomputers, obsolescence leads to cannibalization, where new products replace still-successful ones.

Despite a high failure rate, a continuous influx of new products creates a wager economy with higher stakes against lower odds. Apparently, irrational product strategies play a role in brand preservation, serving as visible signals of continuity and renewal. The *bookstore* effect explains how databases derive value from the total data inventory. Structural abundance results in redundancy and excess capacity, which are functional and necessary in the intangible economy. This shift toward abundance influences the value chain, moving it closer to the consumer and blurring traditional distinctions between markets, hierarchies, and networks [7]. This transformation toward interpenetration significantly impacts firms and their relationships. Internal connections within firms weaken, while external links, especially with suppliers, strengthen. Traditional functions vital to a firm's existence are often outsourced or subcontracted. For example, industry leaders like Nike and Dell focus on design and outsource manufacturing. Similarly, the semiconductor industry prioritizes chip design and subcontracting production. The growth of outsourcing in computer services further exemplifies this trend [5].

Software Eats the World

In 2011, Marc Andreessen, founder of Netscape and a key figure in Silicon Valley, introduced the concept that "software is eating the world." This idea conveyed that traditional business models, like physical bookstores, were increasingly being challenged by software-based enterprises such as Amazon. These businesses not only facilitated online shopping but also offered a broader selection of titles, surpassing the limitations of physical stores. Andreessen's central argument, predicting the widespread dominance of software-based business models over their nonsoftware counterparts, has proven true and is fundamental to the ongoing digitalization process. Similar to a new industrial revolution, this shift is marked by the growing importance of intangible assets, primarily reliant on software, often surpassing the value of physical capital in various businesses [3].

Digitalization of the economy means that many tasks in our daily lives can be streamlined through interactions involving humans with machines, machines with machines, and machines with humans. Digital technologies are creating new combinations of cognitive, physical, and mechanical work. Integrating information and operational technology across diverse industries is expected to lead to cost reductions, improved quality, and increased efficiency [8]. As per Bosch's Siegfried Dasch, the future of manufacturing will be characterized by interconnected processes, where virtual–real interactions will enhance productivity. Essentially, the future of manufacturing will involve a dynamic interplay between the physical and digital spaces. General Electric introduced the term Industrial Internet to describe integrating digital technology into all machines and devices. According to General Electric's estimates, the Industrial Internet could potentially save the aviation sector up to U.S.$2 billion annually [8]. This intelligent manufacturing approach applies across various industries, from food and consumer goods to the high-tech sector. The incorporation of networked software into products and machinery will empower businesses in several ways. For example, facilitating machine-to-machine communication without human intervention reduces reliance on human labor, significantly contributing to efficiency and security. Machine-to-machine applications utilize microelectronics and wireless technology to gather and distribute real-time data within a network. Businesses can leverage the Industrial Internet to streamline upgrades and maintenance tasks, thereby improving the reliability and speed of their operations.

As digitalization progresses, firms shift from manufacturing to service sectors, highlighting the need for a comprehensive approach to software development analysis across the economy. Adopting software-based technologies is more a matter of when than if, as most parts of the economy already incorporate such technologies to some extent. Statistics indicate widespread usage of software-based technologies, with most firms adopting them to varying degrees. Investing in software development is similar to a *make or buy* choice tied to digital transformation. While standardized software offers lower initial costs and broader availability, developing proprietary software may yield a unique competitive advantage or pose risks and uncertainties. Both necessity and opportunity drive this decision, distinguishing firms engaged in software development from those relying on standardized software.

As digitalization advances across various sectors of the economy, the role of software development becomes increasingly prominent. The decision to invest in software development rather than opting for standardized off-the-shelf software can be seen in two ways. Firstly, it means calculated risk-taking, driven by necessity when suitable standardized software is lacking or by opportunity when the investing firm believes it can create a superior software-based solution. Even if software development begins as a means to an end within an existing business model, it may evolve into a new business opportunity, allowing the firm to sell software independently. Furthermore, a firm engaging in software development is integral to its digital transformation. To harness productivity benefits from new technologies, firms must experimentally search for complementary innovations, adapting their organization and work processes to the available tools. Software development is a means of tailoring these new tools to the specific needs of individual firms [3].

Addiction and Loss of Attention

As discussed in the previous chapters, the intangible economy is characterized by high scalability and low to zero marginal costs, leading to an abundance of intangible production and supply. In this economic model, businesses find themselves with an infinite number of products but a limited number of consumers. As a result, they must compete for consumers' attention, often resorting to enticing, addictive, and manipulative techniques. Digital businesses, particularly those in social media, online gaming, and e-commerce, frequently offer instant gratification in the intangible economy. Users can swiftly access information and entertainment or purchase with just a few clicks. This immediate reward creates a sense of pleasure, reinforcing user behavior and encouraging frequent returns. Many digital platforms incorporate gamification elements, transforming user interactions into a game-like experience. Features such as likes, comments, and badges establish a reward system that triggers the release of dopamine, a neurotransmitter associated with pleasure and reinforcement. This, in turn, can lead to repetitive and addictive behavior as individuals actively seek these rewards. For example, Robinhood's commission-free trading platform has gained popularity, especially among young users, partly due to its effective use of gamification elements. Gamification involves integrating game-like features and design into non-game contexts to engage and motivate users. Robinhood utilizes intuitive design, colorful and engaging graphics, a reward system, progress tracking, and social features, making investing more captivating, accessible, and enjoyable for a younger audience.

Many businesses utilize advanced algorithms to tailor content and recommendations based on user preferences and behaviors. This personalized experience can be captivating and addictive, as users feel a sense of connection and relevance, prompting them to spend more time on the platform. Social media platforms thrive on social validation through likes, comments, and shares. The desire for positive feedback and social approval can lead individuals to use these platforms, seeking validation and connection excessively.

The prevalence of smartphones and other digital devices ensures constant connectivity, allowing users to access digital services and content anytime, anywhere. This blurs the line between work, leisure, and personal time, contributing to compulsive checking and use of digital platforms. Additionally, digital platforms can serve as escapism from real-world stressors. Whether through social media, video games, or other online activities, individuals may turn to digital experiences to cope with challenges or find temporary relief. This escapism can result in excessive use and dependency. Content discovery algorithms play a role in creating a personalized and endless feed of content, keeping users engaged for extended periods. Some digital businesses incorporate emotional storytelling in their content or advertising to establish a deeper connection with users.

Meta (Facebook) has faced criticism for employing strategies that can contribute to addictive behaviors, especially among children. Concerns include extended screen time, sleep disruption, and potential addiction. Children may develop a dependency on social validation, influencing their self-esteem and well-being. The gamified aspects of platforms may be enticing, leading to repetitive use as children strive to earn rewards. Attention deficit hyperactivity disorder (ADHD) is a growing neurodevelopmental disorder that could be caused or exacerbated by gamification and information overload. Prolonged screen time may also contribute to sedentary behaviors, impacting physical health.

Surveillance, Intrusion, and Invasion

Shoshana Zuboff, an American social psychologist, coined the term *surveillance capitalism* to highlight the intrusive and invasive character of businesses in intangible economy [9]. In an intangible economy, corporations' business model is to collect vast amounts of personal data from their users constantly. These data include online behaviors, preferences, location information, and social connections. The collected data are analyzed using advanced algorithms and AI to create predictive models of individual and collective behavior. This predictive power is utilized to anticipate users' needs, preferences, and actions. Companies use behavioral predictions to serve users personalized and highly targeted ads. Intrusive practices may involve the constant surveillance and tracking of users across various online activities. This can include monitoring website visits, app usage, and interactions on social media platforms. Invasive practices go beyond mere data collection and involve actions that can potentially infringe on user privacy. This may include accessing personal communication, reading e-mails, monitoring private messages, and recording conversations. Digital businesses may share user data with third-party entities, such as advertisers or analytics companies. Invasive practices may lead to security vulnerabilities, increasing the risk of data breaches. If sensitive user information is not adequately protected, it can be accessed by unauthorized parties, resulting in significant privacy and security concerns. Psychological profiling often relies on analyzing user data to create profiles that can be used for targeted advertising, content recommendations, and personalized experiences. Surveillance creates a power imbalance between those who collect and control the data and those whose data are being collected. This imbalance raises ethical privacy concerns and ultimately benefits corporations and the detriment of citizens. Furthermore, there are serious concerns about the impact of targeted content on elections, public opinion, and social cohesion.

The United States has a relatively lax regulatory framework compared to Europe, with a more market-driven approach. Major tech companies based in the United States, such as Google, Facebook (Meta), and Amazon, dominate the global tech landscape and often operate on the surveillance model, collecting extensive user data for targeted advertising. The European Union has taken a more stringent approach to data privacy by implementing the General Data Protection Regulation (GDPR). GDPR empowers individuals with greater control over their data and imposes strict requirements on companies regarding data collection, processing, and storage. By contrast, the government plays a significant role in surveillance practices in China. The Chinese government has implemented extensive surveillance systems, such as facial recognition technology and the social credit system, to monitor citizens.

Distortion of Reality, Truth, and Our Existence

In an intangible economy, the generation of value and wealth revolves around manipulating and leveraging ideas, knowledge, and information instead of tangible assets or physical goods. This model starkly contrasts with agrarian and industrial economies, where wealth predominantly stems from producing and exchanging agricultural products or manufactured goods. Consequently, the production of intangibles, or the *manipulation of ideas*, holds significant implications for concepts such as information, knowledge, the human mind, perception, imagination, reality, and even the notion of truth itself.

Innovation is a driving force in the intangible economy, with companies actively seeking to disrupt traditional ways of life. Industries such as information technology, finance, health care, and entertainment thrive on creating, applying, and disseminating knowledge. However, in this process, they may reinvent or revolutionize basic concepts. For example, Amazon.com revolutionized traditional notions such as books, bookshops, authors, publishers, readers, and libraries, while Facebook transformed fundamental concepts related to human communication, relationships, community, and friendship.

The Metaverse is a virtual reality space where users interact with computer-generated environments and other users in real time. As the Metaverse evolves, it significantly alters our conception of space and location. It establishes a parallel reality where users can navigate and interact with virtual spaces alongside the physical world, free from the constraints of the physical environment. Thus, Metaverse challenges the traditional concept of physical presence, allowing users to be virtually present in different locations simultaneously, interacting without geographical constraints. Ownership extends to virtual real estate within the Metaverse, fostering a digital economy independent of physical geography and governed by its own rules and economic dynamics.

The convergence of virtual reality, augmented reality, AI, and robotics is reshaping our perception of reality and introducing the concept of hyperreality. In this hyperrealistic environment, illusions are crafted, and distinctions between the real and the simulated become increasingly blurred. These technologies contribute to hyperreality by enhancing sensory experiences and manipulating perceptions.

The use of AI in generating content blurs the lines between authenticity and artificially created content, as machines mimic human-like behaviors and creativity. Deepfake technology, a product of AI, enables the creation of highly realistic and often indistinguishable fake images, videos, and recordings, further blurring the boundary between real and manipulated content. The sheer volume of information produced by AI systems and robots can overshadow considerations of accuracy and reliability.

In a hyper-connected intangible environment, the prioritization of *quantity* over *quality* in information may distort the truth. Notably, Oxford Dictionaries declared *posttruth* as the year's word in 2016, and Collins Dictionaries chose *fake news* as the Word of the Year in 2017 [6]. Posttruth refers to circumstances where objective facts have less influence on public opinion than appeals to emotion and personal belief [1]. Baudrillard [4] suggests that the contemporary world is dominated by hyperreality, blurring or even indistinguishably erasing the boundary between reality and its simulated representation. We find ourselves in a state where what we perceive as real is overshadowed by its simulated or exaggerated versions.

Allcott and Gentzkow [2] assert that fake news, amplified by new technology, threatens open society and can destabilize liberal democracies. The erosion of trust in institutions and the blurring of truth and falsehood can lead to a sense of disillusionment and apathy among the public. In the posttruth era, the democratic process can be manipulated through the spread of false narratives, misinformation campaigns, and the spreading of distrust.

Losing Our Existence

René Descartes' renowned philosophical assertion, *Cogito ergo sum*, conveys the idea that "I exist only as a thinking self." Descartes posited that the mind, or the thinking entity, is the defining factor of our existence. Absent the act of thinking, there would be a lack of conscious awareness of one's being. Our capacity to think and reflect upon our thoughts bestows us a sense of self-awareness, distinguishing us as thinking entities. Consequently, thinking emerges as a defining characteristic of the self and a means of validating one's existence. Through thinking, we acquire knowledge, make judgments, and interact with the world around us. These cognitive processes serve as the foundation for confirming our own existence, shaping our beliefs, and forming perceptions about ourselves and the external reality. Thinking stands as an integral facet of our self-awareness and a mechanism through which we validate our existence and engage with the world.

AI a byproduct of intangible economy harbors the potential to impact various facets of human thinking, education, upbringing, and cognitive activities. AI can process and analyze vast amounts of data at speeds surpassing human capacity. AI algorithms can uncover insights and correlations that might elude human observers. In education, AI can enhance or potentially replace traditional methods by offering diverse solutions and assignments. It is conceivable that AI may supersede specific human cognitive capacities, emotions, empathy, social skills, image and pattern recognition, and language translation. AI may take over numerous cognitive and emotive activities, including higher-order thinking, abstract reasoning, artistic and scientific creativity, and innovation. One could argue that as AI systems grow more sophisticated and proficient in tasks traditionally associated with human intelligence, they develop and possess a form of thinking or consciousness in their own right. *The New Cogito* implies that AI thinks in lieu of humans. Suppose AI assumes the role of thinking instead of humans. In that case, it raises the prospect that part of our identity or even our existence as a thinking entity could be deconstructed and lost. AI thinks; therefore, AI exists, I do not.

Concluding Remarks

As we conclude this final chapter, it becomes clear that the emergence of intangible capitalism triggers significant societal changes affecting various facets of our lives, such as behaviors, values, attitudes, and even perceptions and cognitions. As explored in Chapter 2, the rise of intangible capitalism can be attributed to the transition to a postindustrial society and the resulting cultural shifts. Additionally, the ascendancy of the intangible economy exerts considerable influence across all aspects of social life. These observations lead to the conclusion that intangible capitalism is both a cause and a consequence of postindustrialization and human development. This notable insight highlights the interplay between postmodern/postindustrial culture and intangible capitalism. It emphasizes intangible capitalism as a significant paradigm shift poised to transform conventional business and management practices.

References

Chapter 1

[1]   Andrews, D. and A. De Serres. 2012. *Intangible Assets, Resource Allocation, and Growth: A Framework for Analysis.*

[2]   Balsillie, J. May 19, 2021. "Re-building Canada's Institutional Capacity for Policy-Making in the Modern Economy." Submission to the House of Commons Standing Committee on Industry, Science and Technology.

[3]   Chareonsuk, C. and C. Chansa-ngavej. 2008. "Intangible Asset Management Framework for Long-Term Financial Performance." *Industrial Management & Data Systems 108,* no. 6, pp. 812–828.

[4]   Cohen, J.A. 2011. *Intangible Assets: Valuation and Economic Benefit* 273 vols. John Wiley & Sons.

[5]   Crouzet, N., J. Eberly, A. Eisfeldt, and D. Papanikolaou. 2022a. "Replication Data for: Economics of Intangible Capital." *American Economic Association* Inter-university Consortium for Political and Social Research. https://doi.org/10.3886/E172021V1.

[6]   Di Tommaso, M., Paci, D., & Schweitzer, S. 2004. "Clustering of Intangibles." *The Economic Importance of Intangible Assets,* 73–102.

[7]   The Economist Intelligence Unit. 2022. https://impact.economist.com/perspectives/sites/default/files/eiu_cms_desktop_infographic_19052021.pdf.

[8]   Hazan, E., P.S. Smit, A.J. Woetzel, S.B. Cvetanovski, L.M. Krishnan, and B.B. Gregg. 2021. *Getting Tangible About Intangible.*

[9]   Howes, C. and A. von Ende-Becker. 2022. "Monetary Policy and Intangible Investment." *Economic Review 107,* no. 2.

[10] Madhani, P.M. 2012. "Intangible Assets: Value Drivers for Competitive Advantage." In *Best Practices in Management Accounting* 146–165. London: Palgrave Macmillan UK.

[11] Ocean Tomo. 2023. https://oceantomo.com/.

Chapter 2

[1]   Arrow, K.J. 1972. *Economic Welfare and The Allocation of Resources for Invention* 219–236. Macmillan Education UK.

[2]   Beck, U. 2018. *What is Globalization?* John Wiley & Sons.

[3]   Beck, U. 2009. *World at Risk.* Polity.

[4] Bell, D. 1973. *The Coming of Post-Industrial Society*. NY, New York: Basic Books.

[5] Bell, D. 1976. *The Cultural Contradictions of Capitalism*. NY, New York: Basic Books.

[6] Ben-David, I., Y. Jang, S. Kleimeier, and M. Viehs. 2021. "Exporting Pollution: Where Do Multinational Firms Emit CO_2?" *Economic Policy* Forthcoming.

[7] Bernard, A.B. and T.C. Fort. 2015. "Factoryless Goods Producing Firms." *American Economic Review* 105, no. 5, pp. 518–523.

[8] Braga, C.A.P., C. Fink, and C. P. Sepulveda. 2000. *Intellectual Property Rights and Economic Development* 412 vols. World Bank Publications.

[9] Cahen, F. and F.M. Borini. 2020. "International Digital Competence." *Journal of International Management 26*, no. 1, p. 100691.

[10] Castells, M. 2011. *The Rise of the Network Society*. John Wiley & Sons.

[11] Drucker, P. 2012. *Post-Capitalist Society*. Routledge; Ecola, L., J. Zmud, K. Gu, P. Phleps, and I. Feige. 2015. *The Future of Mobility: Scenarios for China in 2030*. Rand Corporation.

[12] Fontagné, L and A Harrison, eds. 2017. The Factory-Free Economy. *Outsourcing, Servitization, and the Future of Industry.* Oxford University Press

[13] Giddens, A. 1991. *The Consequences of Modernity*. Blackwell, Oxford.

[14] Haskel, J. and S. Westlake. 2018. *Capitalism Without Capital: The Rise of the Intangible Economy*. Princeton University Press.

[15] Hazan, E., P.S. Smit, A.J. Woetzel, S.B. Cvetanovski, L.M. Krishnan, and B.B. Gregg. 2021. *Getting Tangible About Intangible*.

[16] Inglehart, R. 2018. *Culture Shift in Advanced Industrial Society*. Princeton University Press.

[17] Inglehart, R. 2000. "Globalization and Postmodern Values." *Washington Quarterly 23*, no. 1, pp. 215–228.

[18] Inglehart, R. and C. Welzel. 2005. *Modernization, Cultural Change, and Democracy: The Human Development Sequence* 333 vols. Cambridge: Cambridge University Press.

[19] Jonscher, C. 1994. "An Economic Study of the Information Technology Revolution." *Information Technology and the Corporation of the 1990s: Research studies*, pp. 5–42.

[20] Li, X. and Y.M. Zhou. 2017. "Offshoring Pollution While Offshoring Production?" *Strategic Management Journal* 38, pp. 2310–2329.

[21] Liagouras, G. 2005. "The Political Economy of Post-Industrial Capitalism." *Thesis Eleven 81*, no. 1, pp. 20–35.

[22] Machlup, F. 1962. *The Production and Distribution of Knowledge in the United States* 278 vols. Princeton University Press.

[23] New York Times. 2018. You've Heard of Outsourced Jobs, but Outsourced Pollution? It's Real, and Tough to Tally Up. www.nytimes.com/2018/09/04/climate/outsourcing-carbon-emissions.html.

[24] Penco, L. 2011. "Large Cities, Intangible Consumption and Knowledge Production." *Symphonya Emerging Issues in Management* no. 2, pp. 34–47.

[25] Poston, B. 2009. "Maslow's Hierarchy of Needs." *The Surgical Technologist 41*, no. 8, pp. 347–353.

[26] Schwab, K. 2017. *The Fourth Industrial Revolution.* Currency.

[27] Winthrop, R., G. Bulloch, P. Bhatt, and A. Wood. 2015/2016. Development Goals in an Era of Demographic Change. Global Monitoring Report.

Chapter 3

[1] Cañibano, L., M.G.A. Covarsí, and M.P. Sánchez. 1999. "The Value Relevance and Managerial Implications of Intangibles: A Literature Review1." Proyecto Meritum.

[2] Cohen, J.A. 2011. *Intangible Assets: Valuation and Economic Benefit* 273 vols. John Wiley & Sons.

[3] Daum, J.H. 2003. *Intangible Assets and Value Creation.* John Wiley & Sons.

[4] Edvinsson, L. and M.S. Malone. 1997. *Intellectual Capital—The Proven Way to Establish Your Company's Real Value by Measuring its Hidden Brainpower.* London: Judy Piatkus Ltd.

[5] Helderman, L. and E. Sporken. 2012. "International Revision of the Special Considerations for Intangibles in Chapter VI of the OECD Transfer Pricing Guidelines and Related Provisions." *International Transfer Pricing Journal* 19, no. 6, p. 383.

[6] Inkinen, H. 2015. "Review of Empirical Research on Intellectual Capital and Firm Performance." *Journal of Intellectual Capital 16*, no. 3, pp. 518–565.

[7] Jarboe, K.P. and R. Furrow. 2008. "Intangible Asset Monetization." In *The Promise and the Reality.* 37 vols.

[8] Kaufmann, L. and Y. Schneider. 2004. "Intangibles: A Synthesis of Current Research. *Journal of Intellectual Capital 5*, no. 3, pp. 366–388.

[9] Lev, B. 2001. *Intangibles—Management, Measurement and Reporting.* Washington, DC: The Brookings Institution.

[10] Mouritsen, J., H.T. Larsen, and P.N. Bukh. 2001. "Intellectual Capital and the 'Capable Firm': Narrating, Visualizing and Numbering for Managing Knowledge." *Accounting, Organizations and Society 26*, no. 7–8, pp. 735–762.

[11] Sullivan, P.H. 2000. *Value-Driven Intellectual Capital: Converting Intangible Corporate Assets Into Market Value.* John Wiley & Sons, Inc.

Chapter 4

[1] Becker, G. S. (1985). *Human Capital: A Theoretical and Empirical Analysis, with Special Reference to Education.* University of Chicago Press.

[2] Cohen, J.A. 2011. *Intangible Assets: Valuation and Economic Benefit* 273 vols. John Wiley & Sons.

[3] Blackett, T., B. Boad, P. Cowper, and S. Kumar. 1999. "The Future of Co-Branding." In *Co-Branding: The Science of Alliance,* 113–123. London: Palgrave Macmillan UK.

[4] Gu, F. and B. Lev. 2001. *Markets in Intangibles: Patent Licensing. Available at SSRN 275948.*

[5] Haskel, J. and S. Westlake. 2018. *Capitalism Without Capital: The Rise of the Intangible Economy.* Princeton University Press.

[6] Hetherington, K. 1994. "The Contemporary Significance of Schmalenbach's Concept of the Bund." *The Sociological Review 42,* no. 1, pp. 1–25.

[7] Kaufmann, L. and Y. Schneider. 2004. "Intangibles: A Synthesis of Current Research." *Journal of Intellectual Capital 5,* no. 3, pp. 366–388.

[8] Marr, B. 2012. *Future Value Drivers: Leveraging Your Intangible Assets Using a Five-step Process.* CMA, Certified Management Accountants.

[9] Sveiby, K.E. 1997. *The New Organizational Wealth: Managing & Measuring Knowledge-Based Assets.* Berrett-Koehler Publishers.

Chapter 5

[1] Arrow, K. J. 1972. *Economic Welfare and the Allocation of Resources for Invention,* 219–236. Macmillan Education U.K.

[2] Desrochers, P. 2001. "Geographical Proximity and the Transmission of Tacit Knowledge." *The Review of Austrian Economics 14,* pp. 25–46.

[3] Di Tommaso, M., D. Paci, and S. Schweitzer. 2004. "Clustering of Intangibles." *The Economic Importance of Intangible Assets* pp. 73–102.

[4] Edge, D. 2022. *The Great Transition.* DXC Leading Edge.

[5] Feldman, M.P. 2002. "The Internet Revolution and the Geography of Innovation." In *International Social Science Journal 54,* no. 171, pp. 47–56.

[6] Lev, B. 2001. *Intangibles—Management, Measurement and Reporting.* The Brookings Institution, Washington, DC.

[7] Stewart, T.A. 1997. *Intellectual Capital: The Wealth of O Organizations.* NY, New York: Doubleday/Currency.

[8] Stiglitz, J.E. 1985. "Information and Economic Analysis: A Perspective." *The Economic Journal, 95,* no. Supplement, pp. 21–41.

[9] Teece, D.J. 1998. "Capturing Value From Knowledge Assets: The New Economy, Markets for Know-How, and Intangible Assets." *California Management Review 40,* no. 3, pp. 55–79.

Chapter 6

[1]   Bianchi, P. and S. Labory. 2004. "The Political Economy of Intangible Assets." In *The Economic Importance of Intangible Assets*, 25–48.

[2]   Caligiuri, P., H. De Cieri, D. Minbaeva, A. Verbeke, and A. Zimmermann. 2020. "International HRM Insights for Navigating the COVID-19 Pandemic: Implications for Future Research and Practice." *Journal of International Business Studies 51*, pp. 697–713.

[3]   Cohen, J.A. 2011. *Intangible Assets: Valuation and Economic Benefit* 273 vols. John Wiley & Sons.

[4]   Davis, J. 2015. "Capital Markets and Job Creation in the 21st Century." *Center for Effective Public Management, Brookings Institute. www.Bookings. Edu/wp-content/uploads/2016/07/capital_markets. Pdf* (accessed September 1, 2016).

[5]   "The Rise of the Superstars: Special Report." 2016. The Economist 2016. (accessed September 17, 2016).

[6]   Hamari, J., M. Sjöklint, and A. Ukkonen. 2016. "The Sharing Economy: Why People Participate in Collaborative Consumption." *Journal of the Association for Information Science and Technology 67*, no. 9, pp. 2047–2059.

[7]   Haskel, J. and S. Westlake. 2018. *Capitalism Without Capital: The Rise of the Intangible Economy*. Princeton University Press.

[8]   Hassett, K.A. and R. Shapiro. 2012. *What Ideas Are Worth: The Value of Intellectual Capital and Intangible Assets in The American Economy*. Sonecon, LLC.

[9]   Hendry, J. 2002. "The Principal's Other Problems Are Honest Incompetence and the Specification of Objectives." *Academy of Management Review 27,*no. 1, pp. 98–113.

[10] Huebener, P., S. O'Brien, T. Porter, L. Stockdale and Y.R. Zhou. 2016. "Exploring the Intersection of Time and Globalization." *Globalizations* 13, no. 3, pp. 243–255.

[11] Kantor, J. 2014. *Working Anything but 9 to 5. New York Times.* nytimes. com/interactive/2014/08/13/us/starbucks-workers-scheduling-hours.html (accessed August 13, 2016).

[12] Oke, N. 2009. "Globalizing Time and Space: Temporal and Spatial Considerations in Discourses of Globalization." *International Political Sociology* 3, no. 3, pp. 310–326.

[13] Parker, L.D. 2020. "The COVID-19 Office in Transition: Cost, Efficiency and the Social Responsibility Business Case." *Accounting, Auditing & Accountability Journal 33*, no. 8, pp. 1943–1967.

[14] Reich, R. 2008. "Supercapitalism. The Transformation of Business, Democracy, and Everyday Life." *Society and Business Review.*

[15] Riain, S. 2006. "Time–Space Intensification: Karl Polanyi, The Double Movement, and Global Informational Capitalism." *Theory and Society*, 35, no. 56, pp. 507–528.

[16] Waddoups, C.J. 2016. "Did Employers in The United States Back Away From Skills Training During The Early 2000s?. *ILR Review 69*, no. 2, pp. 405434;

[17] IMF. 2017. www.imf.org/en/Blogs/Articles/2017/04/12/drivers-of-declining-labor-share-of-income

Chapter 7

[1] Allen, J.P. 2017. "Information Technology and Wealth Concentration." In *Technology and Inequality*. 25–41. Palgrave Macmillan, Cham.

[2] Anderson, R., C. Barton, R. Bölme, R. Clayton, C. Ganán, T. Grasso, M. Levi *et al.* 2019. *Measuring the Changing Cost of Cybercrime.*

[3] Campbell, D. and R. Hulme. 2001. "The Winner-Takes-All Economy." *The McKinsey Quarterly 1*, p. 82.

[4] Cerny, P.G. 2021. "12. Business and Politics in an Age of Intangibles and Financialization." *Handbook of Business and Public Policy* 193.

[5] Chareonsuk, C. and C. Chansa-ngavej. 2008. "Intangible Asset Management Framework for Long-Term Financial Performance." *Industrial Management & Data Systems 108*, no. 6, pp. 812–828.

[6] Cohen, J.A. 2011. *Intangible Assets: Valuation and Economic Benefit* 273 vols. John Wiley & Sons.

[7] Daley, J. 2001. "The Intangible Economy and Australia." *Australian Journal of Management 26* no. 1_suppl, pp. 3–19.

[8] Di Tommaso, M., D. Paci, and S. Schweitzer. 2004. "Clustering of Intangibles." *The Economic Importance of Intangible Assets* pp. 73–102.

[9] The Economist Intelligence Unit. 2022. "Open Secrets? Guarding Value in the Intangible Economy." www.eiu.com

[10] "The Rise of the Superstars: Special Report." 2016. The Economist 2016. (accessed September 17, 2016).

[11] Moberly, M.D. 2014. *Safeguarding Intangible Assets.* Butterworth-Heinemann.

[12] Eustace, C. 2017. "The Intangible Economy: Overview of PRISM Research Findings." In *The Economic Importance of Intangible Assets*, 1–24.

[13] Francis, T. and R. Knutson. 2015. "A Wave of Megadeals Tests Antitrust Limits in The U.S. *Wall Street Journal* 18.

[14] Haskel, J. and S. Westlake. 2018. *Capitalism Without Capital: The Rise of the Intangible Economy.* Princeton University Press.

[15] Lundvall, B.A. and S. Borrás. 1999. "The Globalising Learning Economy: Implications for Innovation Policy (Luxembourg: Office for Official Publications of the European Communities)." Problems of Political Sciences, p. 25.

[16] Madhani, P.M. 2012. "Intangible Assets: Value Drivers for Competitive Advantage." In *Best Practices in Management Accounting*, 146–165. London: Palgrave Macmillan UK.

[17] Madhani, P.M. 2010. "Resource-Based View (RBV) of Competitive Advantage: An Overview." In *Resource-Based View: Concepts And Practices*, P. Madhani, eds. 3–22.

[18] Nakamura, L. 2012. "Investing in Intangibles: Is a Trillion Dollars Missing From the Gross Domestic Product? 1. *Intellectual Capital for Communities*, 71–85. Routledge.

[19] Prahalad, C.K. and G. Hamel. 1990. "The Core Competence." *Harvard Business Review*.

[20] U.S. Economic Census. 2021. www.census.gov/programs-surveys/ economic-census.html

[21] Rikap, C. 2021. *Capitalism, Power, and Innovation: Intellectual Monopoly Capitalism Uncovered*. Routledge.

[22] Yeganeh, H. 2019. "An Analysis of Emerging Trends and Transformations in Global Healthcare." *International Journal of Health Governance 24*, no. 2, pp. 169–180.

Chapter 8

[1] Ashton, R.H. 2005. "Intellectual Capital and Value Creation: A Review." *Journal of Accounting Literature* pp. *24*, 53.

[2] Cañibano, L., M.G.A. Covarsí, and M.P. Sánchez. 1999. "The Value Relevance and Managerial Implications of Intangibles: A Literature Review1." *Proyecto Meritum*.

[3] Cohen, J.A. 2011. *Intangible Assets: Valuation and Economic Benefit*, 273 vols. John Wiley & Sons.

[4] Eustace, C. 2017. "The Intangible Economy: Overview of PRISM Research Findings." In *The Economic Importance of Intangible Assets*, 1–24.

[5] Goldfinger, C. 2000. "Intangible Economy and Financial Markets." *Communications & Strategies 40*, no. 4, pp. 59–89.

[6] Haskel, J. and S. Westlake. 2018. *Capitalism Without Capital: The Rise of The Intangible Economy*. Princeton University Press.

[7] Hemmer, T. and E. Labro. 2008. "On the Optimal Relation Between the Properties of Managerial and Financial Reporting Systems." *Journal of Accounting Research 46*, no. 5, pp. 1209–1240.

[8] Hunter, L., E. Webster, and A. Wyatt. 2012. "Accounting for Expenditure on Intangibles." *Abacus 48,* no. 1, pp. 104–145.

[9] "Goodwill Impairment Studies." 2022. Kroll. Duff & Phelps. Available at: www.kroll.com/GWIStudies

[10] Lev, B. and P. Zarowin. 1998. *Measuring Intangible Investment.* https://www.oecd.org/industry/ind/1943381.pdf

[11] Palan, S. 2013. "A Review of Bubbles and Crashes in Experimental Asset Markets." *A Collection of Surveys on Market Experiments,* pp. 197–217.

[12] Smith, D.F. and R. Florida. 2013. "Venture Capital's Role in Regional Innovation Systems: Historical Perspective and Recent Evidence." In *Regional Innovation, Knowledge and Global Change,* 205–227. Routledge.

[13] Thornton, G. 2013. *Intangible Assets in a Business Combination: Identifying and valuing intangibles under IFRS 3.* London, England: Grant Thornton International Ltd.; IFRS. 2016. *Intagible Assests.* IAS, 38.

[14] Wen, H. and S.R. Moehrle. 2016. "Accounting for Goodwill: An Academic Literature Review and Analysis to Inform the Debate." *Research in Accounting Regulation 28,* no. 1, pp. 11–21.

Chapter 9

[1] Anderson, R., C. Barton, R. Böhme, R. Clayton, M.J. Van Eeten, M. Levi, T. Moore *et al.* 2013. "Measuring the Cost of Cybercrime." In *The Economics of Information Security And Privacy,* 265–300.

[2] Baudrillard, J. 2001. *Jean Baudrillard: Selected Writings.* Stanford University Press.

[3] Bhidé, A. 2009. "The Venturesome Economy: How Innovation Sustains Prosperity in a More Connected World. *Journal of Applied Corporate Finance 21,* no. 1, pp. 8–23.

[4] Coase, R.H. 1974. "The Lighthouse in Economics." *The Journal of Law and Economics 17,* no. 2, pp. 357–376.

[5] Forslund, H. and P. Jonsson. 2007. "Dyadic Integration of the Performance Management Process: A Delivery Service Case Study." *International Journal of Physical Distribution & Logistics Management* 37, no. 7, pp. 546–567.

[6] Geyer, R., L.N. Van Wassenhove, and A. Atasu. 2007. The Economics of Remanufacturing Under Limited Component Durability and Finite Product Life Cycles." *Management Science* 53, no. 1, pp. 88–100.

[7] Goldfinger, C. 2000. "Intangible Economy and Financial Markets." *Communications & Strategies 40,* no. 4, pp. 59–89.

[8] Goldman, A. 1982. "Short Product Life Cycles: Implications for the Marketing Activities of Small High-Technology Companies." *R&D Management* 12, no. 2, pp. 81–90.

[9]   Goyal, T. 2001. "Shortening Product Life Cycles?" *Electronic News (North America)* 47, no. 16, p. 46.

[10] Gržanić, M., T. Capuder, N. Zhang, and W. Huang. 2022. "Prosumers as Active Market Participants: A Systematic Review of the Evolution of Opportunities, Models, and Challenges." *Renewable and Sustainable Energy Reviews 154*, p. 111859.

[11] Lang, B., R. Dolan, J. Kemper, and G. Northey. 2021. Prosumers in Times of Crisis: Definition, Archetypes, and Implications. *Journal of Service Management 32*, no. 2, pp. 176–189.

[12] Markovitch, S. and P. Willmott. 2014. *Accelerating the digitization of Business Processes*, 14. McKinsey-Corporate Finance Business Practise.

[13] Oghazi, P., F.F. Rad, G. Zaefarian, H.M. Beheshti, and S. Mortazavi. 2016. "Unity Is a Strength: A Study of Supplier Relationship Management Integration." *Journal of Business Research* 69, no. 11, pp. 4804–4810.

[14] Pilkington, M. 2016. "11 Blockchain Technology: Principles and Applications." *Research Handbook on Digital Transformations*, 225.

[15] Scholtes, K. May 5, 1995. "La dynamique de la croissance des marchées de produits dérivés. Unpublished paper, Faculté des Sciences Economiques et Sociales. Namur.

[16] Teixeira, T.S. 2014. "The Rising Cost of Consumer Attention: Why You Should Care, and What You Can Do About It." *Harvard Business Review.*

[17] Van Bommel, E., D. Edelman, and K. Ungerman. June 6, 2014. *Digitizing the Consumer Decision Journey*. McKinsey Quarterly, pp. 1–8.

[18] Xiong, F., M. Xie, L. Zhao, C. Li, and X. Fan. 2022. "Recognition and Evaluation of Data as Intangible Assets." *Sage Open 12,* no. 2, 21582440221094600.

Chapter 10

[1]   Ahlstrom-Vij, K. 2023. "Do We Live in a Post-Truth Era?" *Political Studies 71*, no. 2, pp. 501–517.

[2]   Allcott, H., and M. Gentzkow. 2017. "Social Media and Fake News in the 2016 Election." *Journal of Economic Perspectives 31*, no. 2, pp. 211–236.

[3]   Andersson, M., A. Kusetogullari, and J. Wernberg. 2023. "Coding for Intangible Competitive Advantage-Mapping the Distribution and Characteristics of Software-Developing Firms in the Swedish Economy." *Industry and Innovation 30*, no. 1, pp. 17–41.

[4]   Baudrillard, J. 2001. *Jean Baudrillard: Selected Writings*. Stanford University Press.

[5]   Goldfinger, C. 2000. "Intangible Economy and Financial Markets." *Communications & Strategies 40*, no. 4, pp. 59–89.

[6]   Hainscho, T. 2023. Calling the News Fake: The Underlying Claims About Truth in the Post-Truth Era." *Philosophy & Social Criticism 49*, no. 7, pp. 786–797.

[7]   Kosko, B. and M. Toms. 1993. *Fuzzy Thinking: The New Science of Fuzzy Logic*. 288 vols. NY, New York: Hyperion.

[8]   Schwab, K. 2017. *The Fourth Industrial Revolution*. Currency.

[9]   Zuboff, S. 2023. "The Age of Surveillance Capitalism." In *Social Theory Re-Wired*, 203–213. Routledge.

About the Author

Dr. Yeganeh is a Professor of International Business and Management at Winona State University in Minnesota. He is the author of six books and more than 60 journal papers. His research has appeared in various journals such as the *Journal of International Management, Competitiveness Review, International Journal of Cross-Cultural Management, Critical Perspectives on International Business, International Journal of Sociology and Social Policy, European Business Review, The Journal of East-West Business, Competitiveness Review,* and *Journal of Strategy and Management.*

Index

OTHER TITLES IN THE HUMAN RESOURCE MANAGEMENT AND ORGANIZATIONAL BEHAVIOR COLLECTION

Michael J. Provitera and Michael Edmondson, Editors

- *The Negotiation Edge* by Michael Saksa
- *Applied Leadership* by Sam Altawil
- *Forging Dynasty Businesses* by Chuck Violand
- *How the Harvard Business School Changed the Way We View Organizations* by Jay W. Lorsch
- *Managing Millennials* by Jacqueline Cripps
- *Personal Effectiveness* by Lucia Strazzeri
- *Catalyzing Transformation* by Sandra Waddock
- *Critical Leadership and Management Tools for Contemporary Organizations* by Tony Miller
- *Leading From the Top* by Dennis M. Powell
- *Warp Speed Habits* by Marco Neves
- *I Don't Understand* by Buki Mosaku
- *Nurturing Equanimity* by Michael Edmondson
- *Speaking Up at Work* by Ryan E. Smerek
- *Living a Leadership Lifestyle* by Ross Emerson
- *Business Foresight* by Tony Grundy

Concise and Applied Business Books

The Collection listed above is one of 30 business subject collections that Business Expert Press has grown to make BEP a premiere publisher of print and digital books. Our concise and applied books are for...

- Professionals and Practitioners
- Faculty who adopt our books for courses
- Librarians who know that BEP's Digital Libraries are a unique way to offer students ebooks to download, not restricted with any digital rights management
- Executive Training Course Leaders
- Business Seminar Organizers

Business Expert Press books are for anyone who needs to dig deeper on business ideas, goals, and solutions to everyday problems. Whether one print book, one ebook, or buying a digital library of 110 ebooks, we remain the affordable and smart way to be business smart. For more information, please visit www.businessexpertpress.com, or contact sales@businessexpertpress.com.

www.ingramcontent.com/pod-product-compliance
Lightning Source LLC
Chambersburg PA
CBHW061327220326
41599CB00026B/5066